The Official
Where in the World is
Carmen Sandiego?®
Clue Book

THE OFFICIAL
WHERE IN THE
WORLD
IS CARMEN SANDIEGO?®

CLUE BOOK

BY RUSEL DeMARIA

Based on the computer software
created by **Brøderbund**® Software, Inc.

HarperTrophy®
A Division of HarperCollins*Publishers*

Much of this book was created with the help of
Alex Uttermann and Jim Rintoul. Thanks to both of you for all
the wonderful help. You both deserve as much credit as I.

I want to thank Ken Goldstein, Andrew Pedersen, Todd Arnold,
and Alan Wasserman at Brøderbund
for their help. At Waterside Productions, thanks to everyone,
especially Bill Gladstone and David Fugate.

CONTENTS

FOREWORD

Playing this computer game is a very special journey. You'll travel around the world and never leave your desk. You'll question suspects who will give you very cryptic clues. And as you decipher their clues, you'll discover something unusual—that you're learning a little bit about the countries and cultures of the many places you visit.

As this happens, that all-important question will come leaping into your mind: Where in the World *is* Carmen Sandiego?

Chances are, you're well on your way to finding her. After all, you've already got this book in your hands. And it's a valuable resource. Not only will it make playing Carmen Sandiego more of a group activity, it will make it more fun. While one person clicks the mouse, someone else can read the clues. And someone else can look up the answers. Perhaps *you*, since you have the book. (Remember, you can always go back to mouse duty, perhaps after you are promoted to Super Sleuth.)

But be warned: even as a group activity, catching criminals as devious as Carmen is no small task. Of course this book will help. But it will no more do the hard work of clue solving for you than it will steal the fun of learning a little geography.

What's that, you ask? The *fun* of learning geography? Can a computer game really both entertain and educate? Can putting every member of the Villains' International League of Evil behind bars really be a family affair?

It's your turn to find out. This is your chance to pin on your ACME badge, get your assignment from The Chief, and show your family that you know the difference between Mount Fuji and Mount Kilimanjaro. (Or that you will know the difference, just as soon as you look it up.)

It's been a rare pleasure to create Carmen Sandiego software with all the talented programmers, artists, sound designers, writers, musicians, and producers here at Brøderbund. Our hope is that you and your family will soon be sharing that pleasure as you play Where in the World is Carmen Sandiego?—and even learn a little geography. The Journey is the Reward.

Ken Goldstein
Executive Publisher, Brøderbund Software

THE GUMSHOE PRIMER

Greetings, Gumshoe!

So, you want to be an ACME detective and track down the world's most elusive thief, Carmen Sandiego? That's pretty ambitious. Surely you know that Carmen and her gang of crooked compadres have filched some of the world's greatest treasures, and that they can be very tricky. You'll have to keep your wits sharp and your eyes peeled to stay on Carmen's trail. But before you can even come close, you'll have to nab her V.I.L.E. villains, one by one. They keep their leader well protected!

You'll start out as a Rookie (that's okay, even The Chief was a Rookie once!). Next thing you know, you'll be an Investigator. A couple more arrests and you'll be an Inspector, then a Detective. Keep in mind that the more cases you solve and the more crooks you capture, the quicker you'll be promoted. You'll be a top-ranked Super Sleuth in no time!

Before you get started, here are some special tips that will help you be a truly effective ACME detective.

A FEW PERTINENT POINTERS ON HOW TO PLAY THE GAME

1. Familiarize Yourself with the ACME Babel-Link Translator.
It's found at the bottom of your screen, and is the most important piece of technology a Gumshoe has. It has four components: the **World Wiz Database**, which you can use to look up information on countries and continents (there's even a glossary in case you come across any unfamiliar words); the **Videophone**, so that you and The Chief can communicate, and so that you can reach the Good Guides (Just the Fax, which stores information that The Chief gives you for use in a later game, is also a part of the Videophone); the **Digisketch**, used to enter the information you've received on a suspect and to issue a warrant; and **Fly By Night Travel** (also called the Travel Globe), where you can choose the next location you want to visit from a list of countries. There is also the Notepad, for saving physical clues and information you receive from tourists to use for later reference.

2. Check the Physical Evidence. As soon as you meet with The Chief and receive your assignment, you'll be on your way to your first country. When you arrive, before you do anything else, be sure to check if there is a physical clue (it's usually a scrap of paper or a book). Do this by moving the mouse to either side of the screen so that you can scan the scene. You should get most of the suspect's description from these pieces of evidence. In fact, for each case there are exactly four items of evidence that correspond

to each of the four traits (other than gender) of the suspect. These are *hair color; height; weight;* and what the suspect is *wearing.* By using these clues, you should be able to obtain a warrant without ever having to say, "Tell me about the suspect."

3. Interrogate (that's a fancy way of saying, "Ask a Question").

In each country, ask one of the tourists where the suspect went. You'll only need to ask one person, then see what you can deduce from that. Pay attention to whether the tourist says "he" or "she." That will usually be your first descriptive clue.

4. Use the Notepad.

The Notepad, the yellow box on the right side of the Babel-Link, is a really valuable tool. It functions as your memory as you play the game. Drag the tourists' answers into the Notepad for future reference, just in case. Drag the physical clues in, too. You'll notice that the clues describing the villain's appearance are marked by a red dot, while location clues are marked by a blue dot.

If you make a mistake and go to the wrong location, check back through the Notepad. By checking the clues you've already collected, you may be able to figure out where you went wrong without backtracking. The correct destination will always remain available on the list in the Travel Globe.

5. Check the Travel Globe (Fly By Night Travel). If you don't know the answer to a location clue, open the Travel Globe and see what countries are among the list of possibilities. This will narrow down your choices considerably.

Countries you have already visited are labeled. If there's a green check mark, that means you went to the right country. If there's a red mark next to the country, that means it's one you visited by mistake. Keep in mind that you won't ever have to go back to a country you visited before on the same case.

6. Open the Database. Assuming you don't already know where the suspect has gone, open the World Wiz Database and read the information from each country, looking for the answer to the clue. Don't use the Find feature unless you absolutely have to (see why on page XIX). Instead, most players use a variety of reference books—*The World Almanac*, an encyclopedia, or an atlas. But you don't have to! This book is all you need—it contains the answers to every clue in the game.

If you do prefer to use the Find feature, check the Notepad for

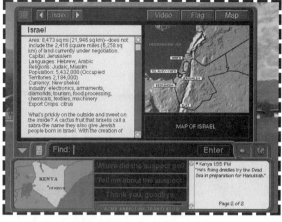

proper spellings of names. The Find feature is very literal, which means it will search for exactly what you type in—so be careful. Also, sometimes a word will appear only in singular form or only in plural. For instance, if you're searching for "llamas," also search for "llama." Be careful, though. Each search costs you battery power.

If one location clue is not enough to figure out where the suspect went, ask another question. But once you have determined where the suspect went, don't ask any more location questions.

You can also call the Good Guides to learn more about your current location. Once you've summoned one of them, you can use that same Good Guide for further information another time.

7. Get a Warrant. After you have identified all the suspect's

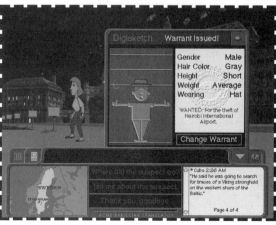

traits and filled in the information on the Digisketch, you should obtain a warrant. You can't arrest a suspect without a warrant!

Remember, if you use one of the Good Guides (you can reach them through the Videophone) to tell you about a city, you can call that guide back later to help you evaluate the information you've entered in the Digisketch.

8. Move On to the Next Location. When you choose your next location you'll know you made the right choice 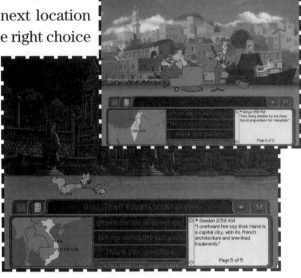 if two klutzy janitors show up, or if Carmen's cat, Carmine, appears. These are always signs that you're hot on the trail of the suspect. At this point, go back to step one—look for clues, question tourists, keep moving to new locations until you catch up with the villain and have obtained your warrant.

9. Make an Arrest. The Chief will sometimes let you know when you've caught up with your suspect. You can also look for the "Stop Thief!" message on the Babel-Link. Find the tourist who matches the description entered in 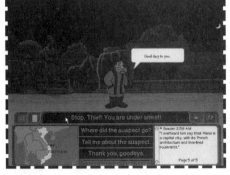 the Digisketch and select the "Stop Thief!" option. If you've made the right choice, you'll watch as the crook is apprehended. The Chief will congratulate you and then offer you a new case. If you make a wrong guess, well . . . try, try again.

Conserving Your Battery

Your ACME Babel-Link Translator, as you've learned, is a handy piece of technology that no modern V.I.L.E. hunter can be without. And that's just what will happen if you run out of battery power. No Translator = No Arrest. So probably one of the most important things a Gumshoe can learn is: *always try to conserve your battery.* Actually, there are a lot of ways you can do it.

It'll Cost Ya (or, Things That Use Battery Power)

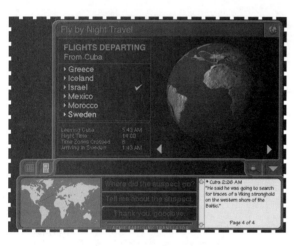

• **Traveling.** Travel consumes the most power of any activity. So make sure you know where you're going before you fire up those jets. You won't get any frequent-flyer miles for going to the wrong place.

• **Questioning tourists.** Hey, that Babel-Link Translator is working overtime with some of those tourists. Think of all those languages . . .

- **Using the Find feature in the World Wiz Database.**

Using this feature makes the Babel-Link think. And thinking is what uses up the battery. So use the Find feature with care when you're on a case. Of course, you can always tell The Chief you just want to explore a little if you're interested in pure research.

- **Issuing or changing a warrant.** Don't issue a warrant until you're sure you've got your suspect nailed. If you're in doubt, check with a Good Guide before calling for the warrant. The Good Guides can tell you if you've identified the right traits. However, changing a trait does not affect the battery. Change traits as often as you need to, especially when you get new evidence.

(Don't forget: you can keep track of how much power you have left. Just keep an eye on the red battery-power level indicator on your Babel-Link Translator.)

Freebies (or, Things That Don't Use Battery Power)

- **Browsing the World Wiz Database.** Feel free to do it to your heart's content! As long as you aren't using the Find feature, your battery will stay charged.

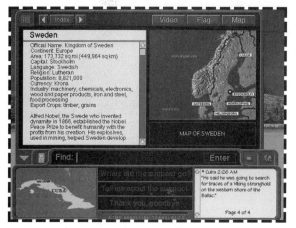

- **Picking up physical clues** (like scraps of paper, or books) and reading them doesn't use any power because the Babel-Link doesn't operate on them.

- **Changing traits** in the Digisketch won't cost you a thing.

- **Looking around the city** might tire your feet, but it doesn't bother your battery.

- **Getting information** from the Good Guides is another free service. Take advantage whenever you like.

- **Using the Notepad.** Do it as much and as often as you like. Your battery will not lose its charge.

Well, Gumshoe, you're on your way to your first assignment! If you work hard and follow this advice, Carmen and her cronies will be making license plates in the Big House before you know it.

Good luck and good sleuthing!

HOW TO USE THIS BOOK

Y ou've just received your first assignment from The Chief, and you're ready to nab that first villain. But wait—you don't know the answer to the clue one of the tourists just gave you. What's a Gumshoe to do?

You can always use the World Wiz Database and read the information on each country. But that takes so long! And using the "Find" feature takes up battery power.

That's where this book comes in. It's really easy to find stuff in here.

Here's how:

1. Turn to the index at the back of the book.
2. Look up any word or concept that was contained in the clue and find the page it is located on.
3. Turn to that page and discover which country the thief has gone to.
4. You know what to do now, don't you? That's right—go to that country and track down the crook!

Here's an example. Suppose the clue mentions something called the Acropolis. You would:

1. Open the book.
2. Look up the word "Acropolis" in the index.
3. Turn to page 66.
4. Read what it says about the Acropolis—"Built on a 500-foot

hill called the Acropolis, the Parthenon is a great example of ancient Greek architecture and, according to some, a marvel of simplicity and design."

5. So, it's in Greece. Go to the Travel Globe (Fly By Night Travel) and select Greece as your destination. It's that simple.

What's more—this book can also be used to learn about other countries, just for fun. There are lots of interesting facts between these two covers—not only clues for the game. If you are curious about Turkey, or Singapore, or Argentina, for example, you can read about these places whenever you like.

But for now, hurry up and get back on the case—Carmen's on the loose, and it's up to you to catch her!

AFGHANISTAN

Welcome to the land called the Islamic State of Afghanistan, better known as Afghanistan. Located in central Asia, northwest of the Indian subcontinent, Afghanistan shares its borders with six different countries, including Iran and Pakistan. Three of the neighboring countries were once part of the Soviet Union—Tajikistan, Uzbekistan, and Turkmenistan.

A mountain range that forms the eastern part of Afghanistan, called the Hindu Kush, cuts through this whole southwest part of Asia. There is a slim sliver of the country that meets China, and that part of the Hindu Kush is called the Wakhan Corridor. These mountains also extend into western Pakistan, where a mountain pass called the Khyber Pass connects Afghanistan to Pakistan. Thirty-five miles long, it is famous as the gateway for invasions of the Indian subcontinent from the northwest. The Persians, Greeks, Mughals, Afghans, and even the British used it for this purpose.

It's not easy being landlocked, but Afghanistan is. It's also mostly mountainous. Most of the country, in fact, is over 4,000 feet above sea level! Besides the Hindu Kush, there are other mountain ranges in Afghanistan including the Koh-i-Baba Mountains and the Torkestan Mountains. As you've probably noticed by now, what goes up must come down, and where there are mountains towering as high as 16,000 feet (like the Hindu Kush does above Kabul), there must be valleys as well. In the Bamiyan Valley, considered the northernmost outpost of Buddhism in central Asia, there are two enormous statues of Buddha. The statues date back to the year A.D. 400. There are also beautiful sandstone cliffs north of the town of Bamiyan. Caves in the cliffs contain fresco paintings that are similar to the art found in caves in China.

Although historically Buddhism was practiced in Afghanistan, Islam came to the country in the eighth century A.D. and was adopted over time by nearly all of the Afghanis. Today ninety-nine percent of the people in Afghanistan practice Islam, and it is considered to be an Islamic country. The northern city called Mazar-e-Sharif, or "Tomb of the Saint," was so-named because Ali, the son-in-law of the prophet Muhammad, is said to be buried there. Ali is considered by those Muslims who practice Shi'a Islam to have been an important authority of Islam. He was a caliph, or spiritual leader, who was killed trying to stay in power. The Shi'a believed that his descendants, the 'Alids, are the rightful heads of Islam.

Although it was occupied by many other kingdoms and empires, Afghanistan officially declared independence as a kingdom in 1750. In ancient times, when its name was Ariana or Bactria, it had been invaded by the Mongols under Genghis Khan and the Macedonians under Alexander the Great, as well as by the Persians, the Greeks, and the Arabs. By the time of

Kublai Khan, the grandson of Genghis Khan, Afghanistan was the center of trade between Asia and Europe.

Afghanistan was the site of some empires of its own, too. The ruins of ancient Ghazna are near the city of Ghazni, the only remaining walled city in Afghanistan. These ruins are all that is left of the capital of an empire that reached from Persia to the Ganges River. Mahmud of Ghazna ruled over the Ghaznavids, the first Muslim dynasty in Afghanistan, in the eleventh century. Later on, in the 1300s, Herat was the capital of an empire founded by Timur the Lame. For thirty years his troops of mounted archers conquered land from Mongolia to the Mediterranean. Timur used military tactics borrowed from Ghengis Khan. He was called "the Lame" as an insult by his Persian enemies.

Kabul is the modern-day capital of Afghanistan, and it has been the center of much conflict since it is located in a strategic place in the country—the point where the mountain passes to Pakistan sit. Large areas of Kabul were destroyed in the civil war between a communist Afghan government (supported by the Soviet Union and its armies) and the fierce mujahidin (Muslim "holy warriors"). Soviet troops were sent into Afghanistan in 1979 to keep the communist government in power, and they did not leave until a decade later. Afghanistan wasn't fully free of their influence until 1992, and even today Kabul is still a focal point for battles between different mujahidin.

Afghanistan's population is actually made up of several different tribes of people. Most are Pashtuns, but there are also Hazaras, Tadzhiks, Uzbeks, and others like the Nuristanis and the Turkmen. The languages most commonly spoken are Dari Persian (Farsi) and Pashtu.

Other Facts About Afghanistan

- A chadris is a tentlike garment. In most countries, they are fairly plain and usually dark, but in Afghanistan the women make brightly colored chadris.

- A karakul hat is made from the fleece of the Karakul sheep. The Afghani people have herded sheep for centuries, and the Karakul are prized for their curly fleece.

- The carpets and rugs from Afghanistan are known throughout the world. They are made with the wool of Karakul sheep.

- The city of Charikar is known for its pottery, fine grapes, cutlery, and silverwork. It was a strategic center during the war between the Soviet Union and the Afghan army and guerillas.

- Quandahar is the second largest city in Afghanistan. It became the first capital in 1747.

- Bactrian camels are camels that have two humps. They are used as pack animals, and their hair is used for textiles.

- Maimana, in the northwest, is where nomads trade Karakul sheep.

- Twenty miles southwest of Baghlan lie the ruins of a Zoroastrian fire temple, called Ateshkadeh-ye Sorkh Kowtal. Zoroastrianism is an ancient Persian religion based on the teachings of the prophet Zoroaster.

- Jalalabad is an ancient city in a strategic location. It has been occupied since the second century B.C. The modern town was started in the 1560s by Akbar, the greatest Mughal ruler of India.

- People in Afghanistan spend afghanis to buy luscious pomegranates that are grown there.

- Yaks are found in Afghanistan. They are often raised like cattle, and their hides provide leather.

- The Turkomen are nomads who can be found in Afghanistan, Iran, and Turkmenistan.

ARGENTINA

rgentina is a big place—the second-largest country in South America. The name Argentina means "Nation of Silver," even though silver is not among the country's main exports. Most of the people in Argentina live on the central plains, called the pampas. Throughout the pampas farmers raise cattle and sheep, and real-life cowboys called gauchos live and work on estates known as estancias.

Buenos Aires, which literally means "Good Airs" in Spanish, is the capital of Argentina. While the President of the United States lives in the White House, the President of Argentina lives in a pink one. The people of Buenos Aires refer to themselves as portenos, or "people of the port." You might think you were somewhere in Europe if you walked through the streets of the capital city. That's because most Argentinian families have roots in Spain and Italy, though others trace their origins to France, Germany, Austria, Russia, Great Britain, Switzerland, and Poland. Only about five percent of the population is indigenous to the area.

Besides being a large country, Argentina has some very large landmarks. For instance, Mount Aconcagua, located in the Andes mountain range, is the highest mountain in the Americas at 22,834 feet. Iguazu Falls, which is partly in Argentina and partly in Brazil, is two miles wide, making it the widest waterfall in the world. And Buenos Aires's Avenida Nueve de Julio, or Ninth of July Avenue, is the widest boulevard in the world.

In 1982 Argentina became involved in a brief war with Great Britain over the Falkland Islands (also known as the Malvina Islands). The British defeated the Argentinians, and this defeat led to the fall of the dictatorship that had been in power in Argentina. A more democratic government was formed, and now Argentina's leaders are elected by popular vote.

Other Facts About Argentina

- Rosario is one of Argentina's major cities, located on the Paraná River.

- Carlos Gardel was Argentina's leading composer of music for the tango, Argentina's national dance.

- The Strait of Magellan separates Tierra del Fuego, an island group just south of Argentina, from the rest of the South American continent.

- Cape Horn forms the southernmost tip of the South American continent.

- Sheep herded by gauchos, South American cowboys, can be found all across the pampas—a flat, grassy region in Argentina's interior.

- Córdoba, located on the Rio Primero, is the home of the University of Córdoba, which was founded in 1613.

- The Colón Theater is located in Buenos Aires.

- The Lanin volcano is located in the Lanin State Park near the city of Neuquén, which is situated on the Neuquén River.

- The Valdez Peninsula is a narrow strip of land that extends into the Atlantic Ocean near the mouth of the Chubut River on the eastern side of Argentina.

- The Salado River is located in the northern part of Argentina.

- Río de la Plata literally means "River of Silver" in Spanish.

- Mar del Plata is a city on the eastern coast of Argentina whose name means "Ocean of Silver" in Spanish.

- The Gran Chaco is a lowland area that extends from Paraguay into Bolivia and Argentina. It is one of the hottest places in South America.

- The Patagonian plateau is located in southern Argentina. This windy and sparsely populated area is full of rich mineral deposits and unusual wildlife.

- A typical food in Argentina is bife de chorizo (prime sirloin).

- Mate is a very strong tea popular in Argentina.

- Gauchos are excellent horsemen, and one of the most popular sports in Argentina is polo.

- When they go shopping, people in Argentina need to bring along plenty of pesos.

- *Evita*, the 1978 musical by British composer Andrew Lloyd Webber, tells the life story of the second wife of Argentine dictator Juan Perón. Eva Duarte de Perón, best known simply as Evita, was revered by the economically underprivileged people of Argentina. She helped to raise wages and establish thousands of hospitals, schools, orphanages, and other charitable institutions. Evita died of cancer at the age of thirty-three.

AUSTRALIA

G'day, mate! That's how the Aussies welcome you in the land Down Under—the Commonwealth of Australia, an independent country located south of the equator. Although still considered part of the British Empire and under the rule of Queen Elizabeth II, Australia is a self-governing island nation. It actually is a whole continent by itself, the world's smallest. Located just south of Papua New Guinea (which was an Australian colony until 1975), Australia is one of the countries on the Pacific Rim. It was discovered by Captain James Cook in 1770, when he explored the region's eastern coast. The whole continent was claimed by the English in 1830.

Australia's landscape is rich and varied. It has mountain ranges, great plains (most notably the Nullarbor Plain), rain forests, deserts, and salt lakes such as Lake Eyre. Two thirds of Australia's land is desert, mostly in the west; the center is called the Outback. The Great Dividing Range is the long mountain chain that runs along the eastern side of the island. Most of Australia's people live east of this mountain range because it divides the country's humid coastline from its dry interior. One part of the range, called the Alps, is situated in the southeast part of the country. The highest peak in the Great Dividing Range, Mount Kosciusko, is found in the Australian Alps. It is 7,316 feet high. The longest river in Australia, the Murray, as well as the shorter Darling River, both rise in the Great Dividing Range.

Off the eastern coast of Australia is the Great Barrier Reef. It is a coral reef—the longest in the world at 1,200 miles long—and lies underneath part of the Coral Sea as well as the Pacific Ocean. The Great Barrier Reef is home to beautiful coral and other aquatic life, but it is in danger of being destroyed by the effects of pollution and careless divers.

Across the Bass Strait, directly south of the large city of Melbourne, is the island of Tasmania, another part of Australia. This island lies in the Tasman Sea, and some scientists believe that the earliest people to live in Australia were the Tasmans. They first settled in mainland Australia 40,000 years ago but had to move to Tasmania when the Australian Aborigines migrated to the continent. The original European settlers of Australia were mostly convicts and criminals from Great Britain. The Tasmans were exterminated completely by 1878, just after British immigrants swarmed to Australia looking for gold. There are still a number of gold mines near Kalgoorlie, in Western Australia. Today, the Aborigines make up only about one percent of the population of Australia. Two-thirds of them live in cities. Like the Native Americans in the United States, many of the Aborigines live on the equivalent of reservations. They have been struggling to gain civil rights and the return of their lands since the 1970s.

Australia is home to many unusual animal species that aren't found anywhere else in the world: the emu, for example, is a flightless bird. Although most famous for its eucalyptus-leaf-munching mascot the koala bear and the kangaroo, Australia is home to a number of marsupials. (Marsupials are animals who carry their young in a pouch.) Other marsupials include the wallaby, the wombat, and the Tasmanian devil, which looks somewhat like a raccoon. Additional animal species include that egg-laying mammal, the duck-billed platypus; the dingo (wild dog); the barking lizard; and the frilled lizard. What, you might ask, is a kookaburra? It's a bird whose call sounds like horrible laughter.

Australia today has eight states and territories:

Australian Capital Territory is located on a plain surrounded by the Australian Alps. Canberra is the capital city. Canberra is aboriginal for "meeting place."

New South Wales is the agricultural center of Australia. The capital is Sydney, which boasts a shell-shaped opera house on the harbor, surrounded by water on three sides. Woolongong and Newcastle are close to Sydney. In the north can be found the most beautiful opals in the world.

Northern Territory is the least populated of all the regions of Australia. This is where Uluru, or Ayers Rock, is located, near the center of the country. The largest rock in the world, Uluru is reddish in color and is considered sacred by some Aborigines. Darwin is the territory's capital.

Queensland is the wettest and most tropical part of the whole continent. Brisbane, Australia's third largest city, is its capital.

South Australia is among the driest sections of Australia. Two thirds of its area receives so little rainfall that it doesn't support human or animal life. In the northeast, though, is part of the Great Artesian Basin, the world's largest region of natural springs. Adelaide, the capital, was named for Queen Adelaide, the wife of British King William IV.

The island group of Tasmania used to be known as Van Diemen's Land. Its main island is triangular. It has eucalyptus forests where wallabies, tiger cats, and Tasmanian devils abound. Hobart is the capital of Tasmania, and it is the most southerly city in all of Australia.

Victoria is second to New South Wales in terms of population and production. It remains the strongest Australian state in terms of economic development. Melbourne is the capital of Victoria, and the country's second largest city. It is the world's southernmost urban area of more than 1 million people.

Western Australia occupies one third of the continent. The port city of Perth is the capital, and three quarters of the population of Western Australia lives there. There are gold mines in operation near the city of Kalgoorlie, the site of the 1893 gold rush.

Other Facts About Australia

- Australians spend dollars.

- Rugby and other sports are very popular in the land Down Under.

- The culture and rituals of the aboriginal people are very much alive. The corroboree is a popular dance. One of the best-known musical instruments is the didgeridoo, a long tubelike flute.

- Aboriginal culture is reflected in the dreamtime paintings in Kakadu National Park.

- Sheep ranching and shearing is an important industry in Australia.

- The kangaroo got its name when Captain Cook saw a large hopping creature go by and asked a local Aborigine what it was called. The Aborigine shrugged, and said, "Kangaroo." The name stuck, but actually "kangaroo" means "I don't know" in that aboriginal language!

- The outback is a term used in Australia for any inland area that is far away from centers of population. It is also called the bush or the Big Empty. Bushrangers bushwalk in these areas.

- Australians are known for their colorful slang. There are some funny Australian expressions that are used to express everyday items—like the waltzing mathilda (a sleeping bag and belongings), the billabong (a watering hole), and the barbie (a barbecue).

- When in Australia, consider spending a night at a hotel on Woolloomooloo Bay.

- The Aborigines use a woomera, a special hooked stick, to hurl a spear or dart.

- A favorite meeting spot in Melbourne is Flinders Street Station, the largest railroad station in Melbourne and a Renaissance-style landmark.

AUSTRIA

What German-speaking country is covered with mountains and trees? It's Austria, set in the middle of the famous Alps. This home of lederhosen and eidelweiss was the setting for the Academy Award–winning movie *The Sound of Music*. Almost three quarters of the country is mountainous, and forty percent of it is covered by forests.

For nearly 700 years, Austria was ruled by the Hapsburg dynasty. Vienna, the nation's capital, has been at different times the capital of the Holy Roman Empire and the great Austro-Hungarian Empire. So great was Austria's importance in Europe that it was the assassination of the heir apparent, Archduke Franz Ferdinand, that led to the beginning of the First World War (simultaneously ending the Hapsburg rule). After its defeat in the war, Austria was reduced to a much smaller size.

High in the Alps, Brenner Pass has long been a key location on the trade routes of Europe.

Vienna, once called Orae Favianae, dates back at least as far as the fifth century A.D. Located along the Danube River, it was originally founded by the Celts and later occupied by the Romans. In more recent centuries it has been the home to some of Austria's greatest musicians and composers, including Wolfgang Amadeus Mozart, Franz Joseph Haydn, Franz Schubert, Johann Strauss (whose most famous work is probably "The Blue Danube"), Gustav Mahler, and Arnold Schoenberg. Other great musicians resided in Vienna as well, the great German composers Ludwig von Beethoven and Johannes Brahms among them. But Austria's impact on the world isn't limited to music alone. Many great scientists and thinkers have come from Austria, including Sigmund Freud, the father of psychoanalysis.

Salzburg, the birthplace of Mozart, literally means "city of salt" and was so-named for its salt mines. It is best known for its beauty and its famous music festival. Dating back to at least the eighth century A.D., Salzburg, like Vienna, has seen many rulers, including the Celts and the Romans.

Austria's fame extends to its foods, which include Vienna roast coffee, Wiener schnitzel, and a wonderful assortment of pastries, including the famous Linzer torte.

Other Facts About Austria

- Austrians save their schillings for skiing trips at Innsbruck.

- The Vienna Boys Choir was founded in 1498 and counts among its alumni such famous musicians as Haydn and Schubert.

- The Spanish Riding School (also called the Imperial Spanish Riding School) owes its name to the famous Lipizzaner stallions, specially bred horses originally imported from Spain. The Spanish Riding School is the only school of horsemanship in the world that still adheres to the haute école (high school) of the eighteenth century.

- Vienna's Ringstrasse is a circular road that surrounds the city. The Ringstrasse is lined with monuments, parks, and great buildings.

- Mount Grossglockner, at 12,457 feet, is the highest peak in Austria.

- Kitzbuhel is located in the Kitzbuhel Alps. It is a famous winter sports resort, though it does a busy summer tourist trade as a health resort as well.

- Graz is the second-largest city in Austria. It lies on the Mur River between the Styrian Alps and the fertile Grazerfeld valley.

- Linz is another very old Austrian city dating back to Roman times. It is located on the Danube River about 100 miles west of Vienna. Among the landmarks of Linz is the world-famous Johannes Kepler University, named after the noted astronomer.

- If you like to schuss and slalom, visit St. Anton, a popular Austrian ski resort.

- "Auf Weidersehn!" is good-bye, Austrian style.

BOLIVIA

Bienvenidos a la República de Bolivia! Bolivia is one of the few countries with two capital cities. La Paz, which means City of Peace, is the administrative capital, taking care of the day-to-day matters of the country. The judicial capital is Sucre, a city known for its colonial architecture.

A landlocked nation in South America, Bolivia is found in the Andes Mountains, the world's longest mountain chain. Mount Sajama, the highest mountain in Bolivia, is 21,463 feet high. In the northern section, called the Cordillera Real, is Mount Illimani, another major peak over 21,000 feet. Most Bolivians live on the Altiplano, the "high plane," a plateau in the southwest Andes. The highest major airport in South America can be found there.

Lake Titicaca, the highest lake in the world, stretches between neighboring Peru and Bolivia. The Uru people earn their living by fishing on the lake and make homes, boats, rafts, and sails out of the totora reeds that grow nearby. Mount Acomani ("god mountain") towers over Lake Titicaca. It is sacred to the Indians of the Bolivian Andes.

The northeast lower regions of Bolivia, called the Oriente, are lush, green, and populated with rain forests and many rivers, including the Beni, the Mamoré, and the Madre de Dios. The Yungas—deep fertile valleys—are also found there, east of the Andes. Farmers on the Altiplano grow potatoes and wheat, and herd llamas and alpacas, but in the lower regions they grow bananas and plantains, cassava, beans, cocoa, soya beans, coffee, corn, and even coca leaves. Along the very southern part of the country lies the Banados del Izozog, which is mostly swampland. The Pilcomayo River runs from its source in the Andes above Sucre down into the neighboring country of Paraguay.

The Tiwanaku empire, ruins of which can be found near the southern shore of Lake Titicaca, was the first civilization in this area. The Tiwanakurs were the ancestors of the modern-day Aymaras. Bolivia was populated in ancient times by the Aymara people, until they were conquered in the thirteenth century by the Incas. About one in four people in modern Bolivia are Aymara, and many people are descended from the Incas.

The Incas ruled the area in the fifteenth century and well into the sixteenth, until the Spanish conquistadores arrived and defeated them. The Spanish colonized most of South America, including Bolivia, which they called Upper Peru. In 1825 Bolivia declared independence; the new nation was named for Simón Bolívar, a freedom fighter. At that point in time, Bolivian territory reached the sea, for its land spanned what is known today as Chile. Bolivia also consisted of land that is now part of Brazil. It lost well over a third of its territory in wars during the 1800s.

Modern Bolivia is known for its extensive mining of tin, copper, and silver. There are silver mines near the city of Potosí and tin mines at Oruro, among many other places.

Other Facts About Bolivia

- Santa Cruz, a city in the lowlands, is known for the manufacture of leather products and alcohol.

- Cochabamba is Bolivia's third largest city. The Major University of San Simon is there.

- Inca ruins can be found on Titicaca Island. A temple marks the spot where the Incas believed that their founders, Maco Capac and Mama Ocllo, were sent down to Earth by the sun.

- Bolivian men wear caps called chullos, which have ear flaps.

- Alpacas are pack animals, similar to llamas, that are found in western Bolivia. They are important animals because of their fine, silky, lightweight wool. The coat of the hearty alpaca is also resistant to rain and snow, which makes it very desirable in the Andes Mountains. Sweaters made from alpaca wool are treasured all over the world.

- Tourists spend bolivianos on the colorful textiles that are found in Bolivia.

BRAZIL

Brazil actually borders every other South American country except Ecuador and Chile and occupies close to half the continent of South America. In fact, Brazil is the fifth-largest country in the world in land area and the sixth-most populous. Home of the samba, a dance believed to be of African origin, this former Portuguese colony has retained the Portuguese language in contrast to most of the countries in the region, which are Spanish-speaking nations.

The Amazon River, second in length only to the Nile, stretches 4,000 miles across Brazil through jungles and rain forests that house thousands of species of plants and wildlife. In fact, there are more than 40,000 known species of plants in the Amazon basin, and it is believed that there are still many more undiscovered species. Unfortunately, much of this irreplaceable rain forest is being destroyed to make room for human industry and farming, causing great controversy around the world.

In addition to the Amazon, Brazil boasts some significant landmarks, including the widest waterfall in the world at Iguazu, which it shares with Argentina. The dam at Itiapu is the site of the world's largest hydroelectric plant. And the famous city of Rio de Janeiro (which means "River of January") hosts what is quite possibly the world's wildest party—called Carnaval. Rio also boasts the world-famous Copacabana and Ipanema beaches and the spectacular statue of Christ the Redeemer overlooking the city on Mount Corcovado.

Rio de Janeiro sits at the mouth of Guanabara Bay. The famous point of land that marks the entrance to the city is called Sugar Loaf. Among the many other sights of Rio is the Municipal Theater, which is almost an exact replica of the Paris Opera House. Another ornate opera house was built inland in 1896 in the city of Manaus. Because it is located deep in the Amazon basin, it is called Teatro Amazonas (Amazon Theater).

Among Brazil's chief industries are automobile manufacturing, oil and gas, minerals, and exporting oranges and coffee. In fact, Brazil is the largest supplier of coffee in the world. Brazil is also known for its gemstones, especially semiprecious stones like the aquamarine, amethyst, topaz, and various kinds of quartz. Precious stones like emeralds and diamonds are also found in abundance. Significant amounts of iron, gold, and other minerals are also found in Brazil. The richest area for minerals is called Minas Gerais.

If you want to go shopping in Rio, visit the opera, catch a soccer match, or sip a cold mango juice, you'll want to pack your pockets with cruzeiros.

Other Facts About Brazil

- São Paulo is Brazil's largest and most populated city. Located right on the Tropic of Capricorn, this industrious city is sometimes referred to as "the locomotive that pulls the rest of Brazil."

- Rio de Janeiro was the capital of Brazil until 1960, when the capital was moved to Brasília, in the country's interior. The idea of a capital located inland was first suggested in the 1700s, but it wasn't until more than two hundred years later that Brasília was built and the capital was actually moved.

- Pelé, certainly the most popular soccer player in history, comes from Brazil.

- During Carnaval, prize-winning samba schools display their art at Rio's Sambadrome.

- The city of Belém is located on the vast Amazon delta, near the mouth of the Amazon, and is considered the entry port for Amazonian trade and travel.

- The city of Recife, located at the confluence of the Capibaribe and Beberibe rivers, is known as the "Venice of Brazil" because it is crossed by many waterways and bridges.

- The capital of the Brazilian state of Bahia is Salvador, but it was once called Bahia Bay, which is how the state got its name.

- Maceió is the capital of the state of Alagoas, which is named for its many lakes. (Lagoas means "lakes.")

- The city of Belo Horizonte was the first of Brazil's "planned cities." As the capital of Minas Gerais, it was originally named Cidade de Minas. Because it is set atop a wide plateau with spectacular views of the surrounding country, its name was changed in 1901. Belo Horizonte means "beautiful horizons."

- Curitiba is the capital of the Brazilian state of Paraná.

- Fortaleza is a port city in northern Brazil that took its name from a nearby Portuguese fort. It is the capital of the state of Ceará.

- Mato Grosso is one of the states of Brazil that does not have access to the sea.

- The sertao is the Brazilian equivalent of the backwoods in the United States, or the "bush" in Australia.

- The favelas are settlements where the poor live. They are the equivalent of slums or ghettos.

- The national dish of Brazil is the feijoada, which consists of black beans with various meats often accompanied by side dishes.

CAMBODIA

The Kingdom of Cambodia is found on the Indochinese Peninsula, between the Gulf of Thailand and the South China Sea. This southeast Asian nation borders Thailand, Vietnam, and Laos. It used to be known as the Khmer Republic and later as Kampuchea.

Although much of the Indochinese Peninsula is mountainous, Cambodia is a mostly flat country. The Mekong River runs through an enormous flat plain that is surrounded by hills. The longest river in Southeast Asia, it drains more than 313,000 square miles of land. The Mekong basin receives drainage from three sources: the Khorat Plateau of Thailand, most of Cambodia's land, and the Cordillera in Laos and Vietnam. The Mekong flows from China, forms the border between Myanmar (Burma) and Laos, then goes through Laos, Cambodia, and Vietnam. It finally flows into the South China Sea from the wide delta in Vietnam. It floods every year and provides Cambodia with rich, fertile land.

There are a few mountain ranges found in Cambodia, including the Dangrek Mountains, the Elephant Mountains, and the Cardamomes Range, also called the Cardamom Mountains. Phnom Aural, the highest mountain in the country, is in this range, along the western side of the country.

Koh Kong (or Kong Island) lies in the Gulf of Thailand, to the west of mainland Cambodia.

From the ninth to the thirteenth centuries, Cambodia was the center of the enormous Khmer Empire, which included all the land of modern Cambodia, Thailand, Laos, and southern Vietnam. During that time, the Khmers built the major landmark in Cambodia, the Angkor Wat. It is a sprawling and magnificent stone temple complex, one tower of which is said to represent Mount Meru, a mystical mountain of Buddhist myth (and of other spiritual paths). Ninety percent of the population of modern Cambodia is Khmer, with a small number of Vietnamese and Chinese people making up the other ten percent. The Khmer have their own language and unique alphabet. Khmer is the offical language of Cambodia, although French is also widely spoken.

The French controlled Cambodia from 1863 until the Cambodians achieved independence in 1953. Prince Norodom Sihanouk was the nation's king from 1941 to 1955 and the official head of state from 1960. Sihanouk kept the country neutral through the Vietnam War, but he was exiled in 1970, when civil war broke out between the government and the small communist group known as the Khmer Rouge. The Khmer Rouge seized the city of Phnom Penh and evacuated its residents in 1975. Cambodia suffered many years of civil war during the 1970s and the 1980s, as well as border fighting with Vietnam. A brutal communist regime run by the Khmer Rouge ruled

Cambodia until 1979 when Vietnamese forces invaded Cambodia and overthrew the Khmer Rouge. This Vietnamese-backed regime governed Cambodia until 1989. In 1991 a peace treaty was signed. Two years later Sihanouk was officially re-instated as the king.

Because of all the wars in the region, Cambodia is the least successful of the countries in this region of Southeast Asia. Most of the land is not suitable for farming, but Cambodians do raise rice and corn. They used to grow rubber trees, but most of the plantations were destroyed during the civil war, and very little rubber is actually exported today. The fishing industry is popular in the area, and there are successful fish farms on the Tonle Sap, a large inland lake.

Other Facts About Cambodia

- Phnom Penh, the capital of Cambodia, was founded in 1434 as the capital of the Khmer nation. It was named after the famous Lady Penh, who discovered a bronze Buddha there.

- Kompong Cham is an important port city on the Mekong River. The Chup Plantation was established a few miles southeast of the town in the rich red volcanic soil that was left there.

- Battambang is one of the only towns in Cambodia that has been able to regain its population since the end of the Khmer Rouge's regime.

- Angkor Thom was the original capital of Cambodia, until Phnom Penh was declared the capital. The modern city of Angkor is the site of the Angkor Wat, a temple complex built in the 1100s. It is also the site of the Angkor Thom, another imposing temple, built in the 1200s. Angkor is another word for "temple."

- The town of Kampot is located on the Koh Sla River and was once a major port. It is in an area of Cambodia that supplies most of the salt for the country.

- Pursat is located on one of the tributaries that feeds the Tonle Sap.

- Riel is the currency that Cambodians spend on such things as clothes made of ramie, a soft and strong fabric similar to linen, and kapok, a cottonlike fiber sometimes called silk cotton.

- Mondul Kiri is a province along the northeast border of Cambodia.

CANADA

C anada, the second-largest country in the world, is the land of a million lakes. Lake Superior and Lake Huron, which are shared with the United States, and Great Bear and Great Slave lakes are four of the largest eleven lakes in the world.

Although most of Canada is English-speaking, there are two national languages. Residents of the eastern province of Quebec, notably the cities of Montreal and Quebec, speak Québécois, a dialect of French. In fact, the Canadian dollar has both French and English words on it. For instance, the ten dollar note has the word *dix* on it, which means "ten" in French.

Much of Canada's vast territory, which stretches from the northern border of the United States to well above the Arctic Circle, is wilderness. More than a third of the country as a whole is covered by forests. This is the home of herds of caribou and moose, as well as seals and many other creatures.

The original settlers of Canada were the ancestors of Native American tribes who made their way over land bridges more than 30,000 years ago. After them came the Inuit (Eskimos). Europeans first discovered the fishing grounds off eastern Canada in the late 1400s, although Montreal was not founded until 1642.

Ottawa is the capital of Canada, but the country's largest cities are Toronto, Montreal, and Vancouver. The economy of Canada depends largely on trade with the United States, and its major exports are oil, gas, and wheat.

Other Facts About Canada

- Sir George Arthur French was the founder of the North West Mounted Rifles in 1873, which later became the North West Mounted Police, then the Royal North West Mounted Police, and finally the Royal Canadian Mounted Police—better known to the world as the Mounties.

- The CN Tower in Toronto is the tallest building in North America.

- If you're traveling from east to west on the trans-Canadian railway, you'll want to get off at Vancouver's Pacific Central Station.

- Named after the Native American word for a local red berry, *Missask-guah-too-min*, Saskatoon is located in Saskatchewan, which got its name from the Native American word for "rapid river," *Kis-is-ska-tches-wan*.

- Winnipeg is located about sixty miles north of the American state of Minnesota. It is the capital of the province of Manitoba.

- Once a gold rush town and the capital of the northern Yukon Territories, Dawson is now a part of the Klondike Gold Rush International Historic Park. Among its former residents are writers Jack London and Robert W. Service, who might have been seen panning for gold back in the late 1800s.

- Moose Jaw probably got its name from the shape of the Moose Jaw River. It is located in south-central Saskatchewan.

- The city of Halifax lies on Halifax Harbor and is the capital of Nova Scotia. Like Halifax County in north California, Halifax was named after George Montague Dunk, the second earl of Halifax.

- The Grand Banks is a part of the continental shelf that extends south-southeast of Newfoundland. It is an extensive international fishing area rich in cod, haddock, herring, and other cold-water fish.

- The St. Lawrence River is one of the longest rivers in Canada and forms part of the border between the United States and Canada. Both Quebec City and Montreal are located along the St. Lawrence.

- Formed from two cities originally designed to serve as military and air ferrying bases for the United States, Happy Valley–Goose Bay is located in the south-central portion of the Labrador peninsula.

- Niagara Falls is a world-class tourist attraction. Lying partially in Canada and partially in the United States, this huge waterfall has long been a favorite destination for tourists, honeymooning couples, and daredevils who try—often unsuccessfully—to ride the falls in a barrel or walk across them on a tightrope.

- British Columbia is the westernmost province in Canada. It stretches from the U.S. border up to Alaska. Vancouver is the largest city in British Columbia.

- Hudson Bay was named after explorer Henry Hudson, who was seeking a passage to Asia when he found this huge inland sea. If you look on a map, you'll see that the bay takes up a lot of space in Canada's northeast territories.

- The Northwest Territories encompass more than 1.3 million square miles and stretch across northern Canada and into the Arctic Circle. There are thousands of islands in the Northwest Territories, including Victoria Island to the west and Baffin Island to the east.

- Baffin Island was believed to have been visited by Norse explorers in the eleventh century.

- Archaeological excavations have revealed that the Vikings visited

Newfoundland as early as A.D. 1000—almost 500 years before the Europeans discovered it. With rich fishing areas, Newfoundland is also an important transportation and communication link between North America and Europe. The island of Newfoundland constitutes nearly three quarters of the total area of the province.

- The Labrador Sea is located between Labrador, Canada, and Greenland. It connects with Baffin Bay and through the Hudson Strait to Hudson Bay. If you are ever on the Labrador Sea, look out for icebergs!

- Located in Lake Superior in west-central Ontario, Thunder Bay is thirty-five miles long and fifteen miles wide.

- Victoria Day is one of the national holidays of Canada. It is celebrated on the last Monday before May 25, in observance of the birthday of Queen Victoria.

- Ice hockey is one of the most popular sports in Canada.

- A popular souvenir for tourists in northern Canada is a soapstone carving of a seal or a bear.

- Commissioned by King Francis I of France in the mid-1500s to explore the "northern lands," Jacques Cartier traveled along the North American coast and the St. Lawrence River. His exploration was the probable basis for French claims to Canada. Cartier is thought to have sailed to Brazil as well.

CHILE

H ola! The Republic of Chile is one of the skinniest countries in the world. It is only 100 to 250 miles across. This South American nation is found high up in the Andes Mountains. The Ojos del Salado, at 22,539 feet, is the tallest mountain in Chile. It can be found in the northern end of Chile, not far from the almost totally rainless Atacama Desert. The northern parts of Chile are hot and dry, while the southern parts are rainy, cool, and forested. (It's only really chilly in southern Chile.) It is such a long country that the climate changes from north to south! Chile even claims lands in Antarctica.

Although there are some volcanoes near Antofagasta in the north, there are many more active volcanoes in the south of Chile.

The western border of Chile is the Pacific Ocean, and the coastline is 2,650 miles long. The southernmost part of Chile is formed by a group of islands. The Strait of Magellan separates this archipelago, called Tierra del Fuego (which means "Land of Fire"), from the mainland. The largest island, Tierra del Fuego, has the same name as the archipelago. It was discovered by Magellan in 1520 and named the Land of Fire because so many bonfires were built there by the local Indians. Half of it belongs to Argentina.

Since Chile is so skinny and the rivers run from east (near the Andes) to west (toward the Pacific Ocean), most of the major rivers are short. The Bio-Bio crosses the whole country and makes a huge valley in the Andes that can be crossed through easily.

Chile's wildlife includes the condor, alpaca, chinchilla, vicuna, llama, puma, Andean huemul (a type of deer), and the Andean cat. There are even penguins in its reaches near the Antarctic. Llamas are used as pack animals in the mountains, and alpacas are prized for their wool. Many colorful garments and hats are made out of alpaca wool.

Easter Island is a small island off of Chile that has a total area of sixty-three square miles. You could drive across it in about an hour! The island was formed by underwater volcanoes. The famous stone totems at Easter Island were erected A.D. 1000– 1600 by indigenous peoples, who were probably descendents of the Polynesians or the Marquesas. Many of the people who lived on Easter Island were carried off by Peruvian raiders in the 1600s. The island was discovered by the Europeans in the late 1700s.

Chile has the world's largest copper reserves, the second largest reserve of lithium, and many other metals and minerals, including precious gems like lapis lazuli.

Santiago is the capital city of Chile and is located in the center of the country. It was destroyed in 1645 by earthquakes. There are still many earthquakes in Chile.

The major port cities are Antofagasta, Arica, and Valparaiso. All three cities are in the northern half of the country on the Pacific Ocean.

Chile's history is similar to that of other South American nations. It was colonized by the Spanish in the 1500s and was agriculturally rich for the owners of haciendas, or huge estates, like plantations. In a war that lasted from 1810 to 1818, Chile gained its independence from Spain. Chile then engaged in wars with Bolivia and Peru to acquire more territory in the late 1800s.

In 1970 Salvador Allende was elected head of state. He was the first self-proclaimed Marxist to run a South American country. His government made economic changes in Chile that were opposed by people who were afraid of losing money. Allende was overthrown in 1973 by Augusto Pinochet, who set up a military junta, or dictatorship. Over 3,000 Chileans died because of human-rights violations under Pinochet's government. Chile finally restored a democratic process in 1989 and voted Pinochet out of office.

Other Facts About Chile

- If you buy wine from the wineries in Chile, you'll pay for it in pesos.

- Famous Chileans have included world-renowned poets Gabriela Mistral and Pablo Neruda (both of whom have won the Nobel Prize for literature), and concert pianist Claudio Arrau.

- The Lake District was colonized by German, Swiss, and Belgian immigrants in the middle to late 1800s. Puerto Montt is an important city in the Lake District.

- The cities of Rancagua and Chillan, as well as a few others, are all in the Central Valley of the country. The growth of these cities helped make this region agriculturally successful.

- Viña del Mar is a resort city near the port city of Valparaiso. The two together make up the second-largest populated area in Chile.

- The city of Iquique used to be an exporter of nitrates; it is now the capital of Chile's fish meal industry.

- Temuco is the regional capital of the Central Nucleus of Chile. The Mapuche Indians, who are actually the Araucanians, live in the nearby countryside.

- The Shrine of La Tirana, on the Tamarugal Plain, draws many pilgrims from Chile, Bolivia, and southern Peru each year.

- Portillo, near Mount Aconcagua, has become the most popular South American resort for skiing in the Andes.

- A large copper mine is located at El Teniente, near Rancagua.

- Near Tierra del Fuego lies the Magallanes province. Punta Arenas, the capital of this area, is on the Strait of Magellan.

- San Fernando is known for its rodeos. There are many huasos—cowboys—in that region of the country.

- The Aymara Indians, who still believe in magic, can be found living on the Titicaca plateau.

- The diablada is a Chilean dance. Dancers wear decorative masks and costumes. People who dance the diablada are called diabladas.

CHINA

The People's Republic of China is the most populous country in the world; after Russia and Canada, it is the third-largest country in terms of land mass. China occupies one four-teenth of the total land area of Earth. The Chinese population constitutes approximately one fifth of the population of Earth, and because most of the nation's people have roots in the eth-nic group called the Han, that makes the Han the largest ethnic group in the world. The main language of China, Mandarin, is spoken by more people than any other language on Earth, though many people also speak Cantonese.

In addition to its size, China is important for its contributions to the world. China was the birthplace of gunpowder, noodles (which they call mein), acupuncture (an alternative style of medicine), and even paper.

China is known for its architecture, rich mineral deposits, and wildlife, including the Giant Panda—sometimes called a panda bear—which isn't really a bear at all. Silk and silkworms are also frequently associated with China. Many gemstones are found in

China. The Chinese consider opal and jade to be particularly auspicious stones, so both are used frequently in carvings and jewelry. Another typically Chinese item is the junk, which is a specific kind of flat-bottomed boat used extensively in China. The Chinese are remembered historically for many things— great paintings, jewelry, temples, and religions such as Confucianism, Taoism, and Buddhism (which originated in India but were popularized in China).

Although China boasts more than 4,000 years of recorded history, the discovery of Peking Man, whose fossilized remains date back at least 350,000 years, would suggest that people have been in China a very long time. In recent times, the government of China has gone from being a monarchy to being a communist totalitarian state.

Even though the communists were in China through much of the twentieth century, it wasn't until just after the Second World War that they gained total control of the country. In October 1949 the People's Republic was formed under General Mao Zedong (sometimes spelled Mao Tse-tung), leader of the communist Red Army. Mao's *Little Red Book* was the basic instruction text for all Chinese citizens during his rule.

Tiananmen Square, or "Gate of Heavenly Peace," was originally built in 1651 in the Chinese capital of Peking (now called Beijing). In its current form, it is approximately 100 acres in area, and each flagstone is numbered to make it easier to position people during parades. The site of many student demonstrations dating as far back as 1919, Tiananmen Square became the focus of the world's attention on June 3 and 4, 1989, when prodemocracy students protested and an undisclosed number were killed. Because of modern communications technologies, including the Internet, the world was able to see what was happening. One of the central figures of the protests, Fang Lizhi, took refuge in the U.S. Embassy and was eventually allowed to leave the country with his wife. The incident at Tiananmen Square was a significant embarrassment to the Chinese government. Other protests around the world center on the Chinese occupation of Tibet, but to date no major international incidents have captured the attention of the press the way the Tiananmen Square massacre did.

Other Facts About China

- Beijing (formerly Peking) is the capital of China and, after Shanghai, its most populous city. Among the attractions of Beijing are Beijing University and the Forbidden City.

- The Forbidden City is the Imperial Palace complex of the Chinese emperors who ruled from 1421 until 1911. It was so named because no foreigners were allowed inside without special permission. In 1949 the complex of palaces was converted into a series of public museums.

- The city known in the western world as Canton has actually been called Guangzhou since the third century A.D. It is one of China's largest cities and is the most important industrial city of southern China. It was the fall of Guangzhou that signalled the completion of the takeover of the country by the communists. Guangzhou is the capital of Guangdong province (also called Kwangtung).

- Officially, Lhasa is the capital of the Tibetan autonomous Ch'u (region) of the People's Republic of China; historically, Lhasa was first declared the capital of Tibet in the ninth century A.D. and again in the seventeenth century. Lhasa is the former home of the Dalai Lama, the spiritual leader of the Tibetan Buddhists. There are many temples in Lhasa dating back hundreds of years.

- Hong Kong, a British colony consisting of several islands off the coast of China and the Kowloon Peninsula on the mainland of

China, is a major trading port and tourist destination. About one third of Hong Kong's total exports are shipped to the United States. Hong Kong reverts to China in the summer of 1997.

- The Yunnan province was first established by the Mongol invaders in the year A.D. 1253. It is now the fourth largest of China's provinces. It is a significant source of agriculture and an even more significant source of mineral resources; among other things, it boasts the largest tin deposits in the world.

- Nanking (or Nanjing) is one of the historically important cities of China. First named in A.D. 1421 during the Ming dynasty, it has served several times as the capital of China. It is located along the Yangtze River (literally, "long river").

- Famous for its lacquerware and other handicrafts, the city of Fuzhou consists of a modern outer city and an ancient walled city dating back to the T'ang dynasty.

- The city of Wuhan is an inland port city more than 600 miles from the ocean. It is also the center of iron and steel production for China.

- The erhu is a stringed instrument bowed like a violin but played vertically. Two strings, tuned a fifth apart, are stretched over a wooden drum resonator.

- The province of Hunan is located where the Yangtze River crosses the Imperial Highway. First founded in 350 B.C., Hunan is a major agricultural center and serves as one of the country's great rice-producing regions.

- Chengdu, one of the oldest cities in China, is the cultural center for the southwestern regions. Among its landmarks are Sichuan University and the Sichuan Opera.

- The term "metal horse" refers to the railroad in China.

- You will want to pack plenty of yuan if you're going shopping in Beijing.

- In 1958 the people's commune system was introduced to China. Each commune, which consisted of a group of people in one community, was organized to be responsible for agricultural and economic development. Over the years there have been many revisions to the structure of Chinese communes. In 1979 most communes were dismantled, and farmers were encouraged to cultivate their own land and sell for profit.

- The Huang Ho, or Yellow River, is China's second longest river— and also the world's muddiest. It is the massive amount of silt that flows from the Yellow River that gives the name to the Yellow Sea, which lies between China and Korea. The Yellow Sea is famous for its fishing grounds.

- Shandong is a province in northern China. Its name, which was first used in the twelfth century during the Chin dynasty, means "Eastern Mountains."

- The Gobi Desert stretches from China into Mongolia. It is 1,000 miles long and 300 to 600 miles wide. On the sparsely populated Gobi, you might find Mongolian nomads living in yurts—tents made of skins or textiles erected on wooden poles.

- The island of Taiwan is located off the mainland of China. Formerly called Formosa, this island is not a part of the communist People's Republic. The capital of Taiwan is the city of Taipei.

- The Tien Shan (also spelled Tian Shan) is a vast range of mountains that separates China from parts of the former Soviet Union. The word shan means mountain in Chinese.

- The Turfan Depression is a fault zone that falls as low as 505 feet below sea level. Although this area can reach temperatures of up to 120°F, with irrigation, the region has become a well-known source of fruits, particularly Hami melons and grapes.

- For followers of the Tao ("path"), yin and yang (literally the "dark side" and the "sunny side" of a hill) represent the opposites of the universe—like light and dark, good and evil, masculine and feminine. These opposite forces, when combined, make up the whole of existence.

- The Han dynasty existed between 206 B.C. and A.D. 220, and was one of the most important periods of unification and expansion in ancient Chinese history.

- P'u Yi was the last of the Chinese emperors. His tragic life was depicted in the movie *The Last Emperor*, directed by Bernardo Bertolucci.

- After the overthrow of the Manchu dynasty in 1911, Sun Yat-sen was the first president of nationalist China. He is sometimes described as the "father of modern China," although it was the nationalist government he founded that was overthrown later by the communists to form the People's Republic.

- The famous dish called Peking duck is a meal in which every part of the duck is served, from skin to bones to head.

CUBA

Havana cigar, anyone? Home of the rumba, the Republic of Cuba is the largest island in the West Indies. There are also several smaller islands nearby that are part of the nation. The Cuban archipelago sits between the Atlantic Ocean, the Caribbean Sea, and the Gulf of Mexico in the island chain called the Antilles. It is just ninety miles south of the American state of Florida.

Cuba is partly mountainous; the rest of it is composed of plains and basins. The Sierra Maestra, a mountain range in the far southeastern part of Cuba, is the home of Mount Turquino, the highest peak in Cuba at 6,578 feet.

There are many bays and gulfs along the southern coast of Cuba—the Bay of Pigs, Guantanamo Bay, the Gulf of Batabano, and the Gulf of Guacanayabo. Just southwest of the Bay of Pigs, in the Gulf of Batabano, there is an archipelago (a group of islands) called the Archipelago Canarreos. The largest of these islands is the Isla de la Juventud, or "Isle of Youth." It used to be called the Isle of Pines, since it is dotted with groves of pine and palm. Other archipelagoes are the Los Colorados to the northwest and the Jardines de la Reina, or the Queen's Gardens.

There were roughly 50,000 natives in Cuba in 1492, when Christopher Columbus sailed to the "Pearl of the Caribbean" searching for gold. The name Cuba comes from the Indian name Cubanacan. Cuba was colonized by the Spanish until 1898. Nearly all of the native populations were wiped out by the Spanish settlers. African slaves were brought in to work on the sugar cane plantations. Slavery was finally abolished there in 1855, nearly a decade sooner than it was in the United States. Today, the population of Cuba is made up mostly of mulattoes (people of mixed racial ancestry), blacks who are descended from the slaves, and whites.

The Spanish who arrived in Cuba were amazed to see the local Indians rolling up tobacco leaves and smoking them. Cuban cigars are famous all over the world today as the very finest cigars in existence. Tobacco and sugar are still the major products of Cuba; in fact, Cuba is the largest sugar exporter in the world.

Cuba fought two separate wars of independence before gaining freedom from the Spanish in 1899. José Martí was one of the heroes of these revolutions.

The target of the first action of the Spanish American War, the U.S.S. *Maine* was sunk in Havana harbor in 1898. American troops didn't leave Cuba until 1902, and the United States signed an agreement to lease a naval base in Guantanamo Bay for another few years. In 1958 former president Fulgencio Batista seized power and set up a junta. (A junta is a Spanish term for a dictatorship.) His government grew harsher and more corrupt, until it was overthrown in the 1959 revolution organized by Fidel Castro. Castro has been the head of Cuba ever since—first as premier and later as president. Cuba is the only remaining communist country in the Western Hemisphere.

Modern-day Havana, the capital city, is like three different cities in one. There are separate areas: Old Havana, Vedado (parts of which are referred to as New Havana or Central Havana), and the suburbs. Old Havana is full of historic buildings, spanning architectural styles from the 1500s to the 1800s. Many of the buildings in Old Havana have been restored. The Plaza de la Revolucion, west of Old Havana, is the huge plaza where President Castro gives his speeches. It is known for the towering monument to José Martí, the leader of Cuban independence. The Museum of the Revolution is one of the many buildings that can be found around the plaza.

Havana was a walled as well as a fortressed city. Several broad avenues and boulevards cross Havana. The Malecón, which runs along the coast, is one of the most beautiful.

Other Facts About Cuba

- Camagüey has become the third largest city of Cuba. It is also the capital city of the Camagüey province. It is important because of the production of livestock, sugarcane, and other agricultural products.

- Cienfuegos, the capital city of the province of Cienfuegos, is one of Cuba's most important ports.

- Baseball is the national sport of Cuba.

- Matanzas, another province, is known for its mangrove swamps (filled with tropical trees and shrubs) and marshes, especially around the Zapata Peninsula. The city of Cardenas, one of the chief sugar ports, is found in Matanzas.

- Pinar del Río, La Habana, and Villa Clara are other provinces of Cuba, all found in the region called the Occidental.

- La Bodeguita is one of the best-known restaurants in Old Havana. It was once a hangout of Ernest Hemingway, the great American author.

- The Hemingway Museum is located in the author's country house in San Francisco de Paula, on the outskirts of Havana. Called "La Vigia," the house is preserved exactly as it was when Ernest Hemingway left on his last trip.

- Cuba has a couple of interesting birds to look out for: the Cuban Trogon, which is red, white, and blue, and the zapata sparrow.

- The Castillo de la Punta is located in Old Havana at the juncture of the Prado and the Avenida Malecón. Originally built in the 1600s, it was renovated in 1863 and is still used by the Cuban navy.

- One of the districts of Havana is called La Rampa.

- "Guantanamera" is a famous Cuban song.

- The San Luis Valley can be found near the city of San Luis in southeastern Cuba.

DENMARK

It has the oldest existing monarchy in the world. It was Hamlet's home in Shakespeare's famous play ("to be or not to be"), and it's the place where Legos originated. Once the hunting ground of Vikings and Norse gods like Odin and Thor, today Denmark is a constitutional monarchy with a parliament like England and extensive social systems providing benefits for the health and welfare of its citizens.

The mainland of this Scandinavian country is located on the Jutland Peninsula, but Denmark is also comprised of an archipelago (a group of islands) to the east of Jutland in the western Baltic. The island group includes Zealand and Funen, which together account for more than a quarter of the total land area of the country. In addition, both the Faroe Islands and Greenland are self-governing dependencies within the Danish realm.

Like Norway, Denmark's seacoast has several large fjords, including the Nissum Fjord and the Randers Fjord. (Fjords are deep inlets with sheer, parallel walls along a coastline.)

Denmark is very poor in natural resources, though the waters are excellent for fishing, especially for herring, cod, and other cold-water fish. The population of Denmark is especially well educated, and the people have a high standard of living. Over sixty percent of the land is still farmed, with more than half of that land devoted to growing wheat, oats, and other cereals.

Denmark has produced its share of famous writers, including the great teller of fairy tales Hans Christian Andersen and the noted philosopher and theologian Søren Kierkegaard. Other famous Danes were Tycho Brahe, a well-known and influential astronomer of the sixteenth century, and twentieth-century atomic physicist Niels Bohr, who won the Nobel Prize for physics in 1922.

Other Facts About Denmark

- Isak Dinesen is the pseudonym for Karen Christence Dinesen, Baroness Blixen-Finecke, who wrote stories in both English and Danish.

- King Canute IV, also known as Saint Canute, was an eleventh-century monarch of Denmark who supported the spread of Christianity through the country. He also attempted to impose sweeping tax reforms and an invasion of England, neither of which were carried out—he was assassinated by angry aristocrats who didn't agree with his ideas.

- The Skagerrak Sea is a rectangular section of the North Sea. It is a busy shipping lane with ports in Denmark, Sweden, and Norway. It is also the location of a key battle, the Battle of Jutland, that occurred between British and German ships during the First World War.

- Royal Copenhagen Porcelain from the Royal Porcelain Factory, noted especially for its cobalt-blue glazes, fluted surfaces, and stylized flower decorations, has been prized around the world since 1775.

- Copenhagen is the capital of Denmark. It has evolved from a small village that existed on the same spot as early as the tenth century.

- The Disney movie *The Little Mermaid* was based on a story by Hans Christian Andersen.

- Copenhagen's famous Tivoli Gardens feature cafes, restaurants, pavilions, theaters, and an amusement park set in a wondrous land of flowers, floodlights, and fireworks. The park first opened in 1843.

- Christianborg Palace is the home of the Danish parliament. Located in Copenhagen, it is a well-preserved ruin of a castle built in the twelfth century.

- The Great Belt is a strait connecting the Baltic Sea with the Kattegat (part of the North Sea).

- Lolland is the third-largest island in the Danish archipelago.

- In Denmark the people speak Danish and they spend kroner.

- The Vikings were a warlike band of Danish, Norwegian, and Swedish explorers who raided and explored throughout Europe —and even to the Americas—from the ninth century through the eleventh century A.D.

- Helisingor (also known as Elsinore) is the home of Kronborg castle, the location of Shakespeare's tragedy *Hamlet.*

- Ålborg has existed since about A.D. 1000, making it one of the oldest towns in Denmark.

- The city of Århus is located on Århus Bay and features a museum of Viking artifacts.

- Odense is located on the Odense River on Funen Island. In addition to being the ancestral home of Hans Christian Andersen, it was once a sacred shrine dedicated to Odin, the Norse god of war. Ironically, it is also the site of Saint Canute's (Knud's) Cathedral, where a shrine to Saint Canute still exists.

• Frederikshavn is an important shipping port located far to the north of the Jutland Peninsula.

• Note: The clue about stealing the Little Mermaid mentions that it may be "a fluke." This is a play on words, as the divisions on the tail of a whale, and, presumably, a mermaid, are called flukes.

EGYPT

S alam Aliekum and welcome. Between the Mediterranean and the Red Seas in the northeast corner of North Africa lies the Arab Republic of Egypt. This desert nation is a mostly Arabic-speaking country, although the majority of the population are of Hamitic, or Afro-Asiatic, origin.

The two major deserts in Egypt are the Western Desert, near the Libyan Desert, and the Eastern or Arabian Desert, which borders the Red Sea. Linking the continents of Africa and Asia is the Sinai Peninsula.

The Suez Canal, one of the most important waterways in the world, runs between the Sinai and the Egyptian mainland. The Suez was built in the 1800s and was opened in 1869. It connects the Red Sea with the Mediterranean. On average, over 20,000 ships a year use the canal, which provides a valuable shortcut from Europe through the Persian Gulf and on to India and the Far East. Though built by a French company, the Suez Canal was owned by the British until 1956. Premier Gamel Nasser was elected president of Egypt in 1956 and ended British control of the Canal during the Suez crisis of that same year.

Nasser was also responsible for the creation of the massive Aswan High Dam, a source of irrigation for Egyptian farmland. The Aswan Dam blocks some of the water that floods from the Nile, creating Lake Nasser and storing precious water there.

The Nile River floods every summer, carrying rich soil from Sudan and Ethiopia all the way into Egypt. It ends at the Nile Delta on the Mediterranean Sea. The Nile is the longest river in the world. Because of the flooding, the land around the Nile is some of the most fertile in the world. Egypt has been called the "Gift of the Nile" for this reason. The areas around the Nile are highly populated. In fact, ninety-nine percent of Egyptians live along its banks.

The first people settled around the Nile about 8,000 years ago. Egypt became one of the first great civilizations of the world. The rulers, whom the ancient Egyptians believed came from the sun, were called pharaohs. Many valuable inventions and contributions to human development came from ancient Egypt. Papyrus, the early form of paper, was made there. Scribes, or trained writers, wrote on papyrus in a picturelike language called hieroglyphics.

There were many famous and powerful pharaohs who ruled Egypt. Many of them erected fabulous monuments and pyramids during their lifetimes. The Great Pyramids at Giza, for example, were built as tombs for some of the pharaohs, and the inscrutable Sphinx rests nearby. The Egyptians believed that the kings would come back to life after they'd died, so they mummified the bodies of the dead pharaohs. Mummies are corpses that are washed, treated with preservatives, and wrapped in layers and layers of cloth. The Egyptian mummies were often put into elaborate coffins called sarcophagi. Many of the ancient mummies have been preserved to this day. The pyramids were stuffed full of the pharaohs' dearest possessions, including treasures, mummified pets, and games. It was believed that when they came back to life, the rulers would want to have their favorite things around them.

Farther on down the Nile, in the hills behind Dayr el-Bahri, lies the Valley of the Kings. This was the burial place of all the major rulers from the eighteenth, nineteenth, and twentieth Egyptian dynasties. There are sixty known tombs in the area—from Thutmose I to Ramses XI. Many of these tombs were hidden deep in the mountain. The only one that wasn't robbed over time was the small tomb of King Tutankhamen, which is on the floor of the valley. It was protected by a pile of rocks left from the construction of another tomb and thereby escaped the notice of thieves. The collection of rich and beautiful treasures that was found in King Tut's tomb is now in the Cairo Museum.

Egypt was known for its queens as well as its pharaohs. The largest tomb in the Valley of Kings belonged to Queen Hatshepsut. Another famous queen, Nefertiti, the wife of King Akhenaton, reigned in the mid-1300s B.C. Two of her six daughters later became queens of Egypt.

Perhaps the best-known queen of Egypt was Cleopatra VII. She was a Macedonian woman—not Egyptian at all. She ruled Egypt with her brothers and her son, Ptolemy XV Caesar. Cleopatra was the lover of Julius Caesar and later the wife of Marc Antony. The last ruler of the Macedonian dynasty that had reigned in Egypt for 300 years, she combined her troops with those of Marc Antony but was defeated by Octavian (the future Roman emperor Augustus). Both she and Marc Antony committed suicide shortly after the defeat.

The Egyptian empire fell apart and was subsequently ruled by different invaders—Asians, Persians, Greeks, Romans, and Byzantines. The introduction of Islam into Egypt came when the Arabs invaded and conquered what had been ancient Egypt.

In more modern times, Egypt was colonized by the Ottoman Turks in 1517, and was taken over by the British more than 300 years later. Egypt wasn't really independent until the early 1950s.

In 1956, the same year as the Suez Crisis, Israel invaded the Sinai Peninsula and took possession of it for the next twenty-six years. Between 1956 and 1982, Egypt was involved in several of the Arab-Israeli wars. Since it has the largest standing army of any country in the Middle East, its opposition to Israel posed a significant threat. Egyptian President Anwar Sadat made an unexpected visit to Jerusalem in 1977 and sowed the seeds of a peace accord with Israel. He was assassinated in 1981. Control of the Sinai Peninsula was returned to Egypt in 1982.

Other Facts About Egypt

- Cairo, the capital city of Egypt, is the largest city in Africa. It is on the eastern bank of the Nile River and has been on the same site for more than 1,000 years.

- The ancient city of Alexandria was founded by Alexander the Great. It was the capital of ancient Egypt until the year A.D. 642. The famous Library of Alexandria was included in the ancient city's academy of arts and sciences. Pharos, the lighthouse in Alexandria, is one of the Seven Wonders of the World.

- Pharaoh Ramses II had two temples built at Abu Simbel. There are four colossal statues of Ramses in front of the main temple. The two temples were moved from the rising waters of the Nile River that resulted from the construction of the Aswan Dam between 1964–66. They were actually taken apart piece by piece and put back together on higher ground.

- Ismailia is a town located right around the midpoint of the Suez Canal. It was founded in 1863 by Ferdinand-Marie de Lesseps, who built the Suez Canal.

- Port Said is located at the northern end of the Suez Canal. It was built on mostly man-made land.

- El Alamein is famous as the site of a battle in the Second World War that marked a turning point in the war. The Allies had their first major victory against Germany when British General Montgomery beat back the forces of German General Erwin Rommel.

- The Great Pyramid of Cheops is the oldest and largest of the great pyramids at Giza. Its original height was 481⅔ feet high.

- The Nile River and its canals provide about 2,000 miles of waterways that can be navigated. You'll often see feluccas—flat-bottomed, two- or three-masted lateen-rigged sailing ships—along the Nile.

- Omar Sharif, the famous actor (*Dr. Zhivago*, *Lawrence of Arabia*), is Egyptian. He is also known as an authority on the card game bridge.

- Naguib Mahfouz, the lyrical Egyptian author, won the Nobel Prize for literature in 1988. He has written more than forty novels and thirty screenplays.

- Al Fayyum was called Shedet in pharaonic times. Al Fayyum was named Crocodilopolis later because it was the center of worship of the crocodile-god Sebek.

- In Arabic speaking countries, a fellah is a peasant or agricultural worker. When you refer to several such peasants, they are called fellahin.

FRANCE

Bienvenue à la France! Welcome to the land of cheese, wine, perfume, and romance! France, the third-largest European nation, lies just across the English Channel from England.

The country is made up of rolling hills and fertile plains. In fact, France is the leading farming nation in Europe. Near its border with Italy and Switzerland lies a particularly mountainous region of France, highlighted by the French Alps. Mont Blanc, the highest point in Western Europe, can be found there, looming at 15,771 feet. The central part of the country is the only really high ground, called the Massif Central. France's southern coast, the Riviera, lies along the Mediterranean Sea.

The Seine River runs through the valley that lies around the capital city of Paris. The Loire River carves out a beautiful valley, known as the Loire Valley, on its way to the Atlantic Ocean. The Loire is famous for the beautiful châteaus, or castles, that line its banks. These fairy-tale palaces were built by French nobility between the fifteenth and the seventeenth centuries. They attract thousands of tourists every year.

The capital city of Paris, built on an island in the Seine River, used to be called Lutetia. Lutetia means "mid-water dwelling" in Latin. Sometimes called the City of Lights, it is also a site of major tourist attractions and historical monuments. Paris is known by its signature landmark, the Eiffel Tower. The tower was built between 1887 and 1889 by Alexandre-Gustave Eiffel. Twice as tall as the Great Pyramid at Giza, it was the tallest structure in the world until 1930.

Paris is also famous for the Arc de Triomphe, the cathedral of Notre Dame, and the architecture of the stunning Opera. In addition, the city is the home of the Louvre, a palace that is now one of the world's greatest art museums. The *Mona Lisa*, the *Venus de Milo*, works of great French painters like Claude Monet, Paul Cézanne, Édouard Manet, Henri Matisse, Jacques-Louis David, and many more can all be found in the Louvre.

The Champs Elysées is one of the most famous streets in Paris. The River Seine runs through Paris, dividing the city into the Right Bank and the Left Bank.

France was known as Gaul, and in the 50s B.C. it was conquered by the Romans. There are still Roman-built bridges in Paris and Roman architecture throughout the country. By the year 486, France was an independent kingdom under Charlemagne. It was one of the dominant powers in Europe throughout the Middle Ages and beyond. French kings continued to rule until the French Revolution (1789–93).

Marie Antoinette, the queen of Louis XVI, was the last French queen. The division between the rich and the poor was growing rapidly in France. Her ignorance of the plight of the poor in her kingdom was painfully obvious in her response when she was told that they had no bread to eat. "Let them eat cake!" she exclaimed. Imprisoned during the French Revolution, she was executed at the guillotine, as were many members of the French nobility.

After the French Revolution, France was a republic. Napoléon Bonaparte, a Corsican general, became the emperor of France in 1804. He tried to expand France by military force, and although by the time he died it was smaller than it had been at the time of the French Revolution, Napoleon was considered a hero by the French.

One famous French king, Louis XIV, was known as the Sun King, "Le Roi de Soleil." Under his guidance, French culture and arts were encouraged to grow and flourish as they never had before. Writers like Jean-Baptiste Molière emerged at this time. Louis XIV built a beautiful palace near the town of Versailles, called simply Versailles. Today the lavish and elaborate castle is mostly a tourist attraction, but some special government funtions are held there.

France has continued to be a cultural center of the world. Many great writers throughout history were French. Victor Hugo, the novelist who wrote *The Hunchback of Notre Dame* and *Les Miserables*, is one of the most celebrated French authors. Other famous writers include philosophers Jean-Jacques Rousseau and François-Marie Voltaire.

France is home to one of the most important cinematic events in the world—the Cannes Film Festival. Many great films have been made in France, including *To Catch a Thief*, directed by Alfred Hitchcock. It was set on the Riviera.

France is also famous for having set standards in cuisine throughout the world. There are over 300 different kinds of cheeses made in France. French wines are some of the best in the world. Early vineyards were begun on French soil with grapes brought by the Romans. Several French cities and regions have locally produced wines named after them. The bubbly wine known as champagne, for example, comes from Champagne, and the red wine known as Bordeaux comes from . . . well, you guessed it, Bordeaux.

The French are known worldwide for their baked goods, including beautiful pastries like napoleons. French breads, baguettes, and croissants can be found in boulangeries (bakeries).

Other Facts About France

- The city of Rouen, in Normandy, is famous as the place where Joan of Arc was burned at the stake in the year A.D. 1430. Joan, or Jeanne d'Arc as she is known in French, was the patron saint of France. A courageous patriot who claimed to be guided by three saints, she was responsible for defeating the English armies at Orleans during the Hundred Years' War. The tower in which she was imprisoned still stands in Rouen today.

- Also in Normandy lies the islet of Mont-Saint-Michel. It is an old, fortified city from medieval times. In A.D. 966 a Benedictine abbey was built there. The city becomes an island when the tides rush in!

- The city of Nice, the leading resort city of the Côte d'Azur (or French Riviera), is on the Mediterranean. It is twenty miles from the Italian border. Nice was founded by Greek sailors, who named it after Nike, the goddess of victory.

- Marseille, a port city more than 2,500 years old, has a history of resisting authority—from the Romans on. "The Marseillaise" is the hymn of the French revolutionaries.

- Marseille is known for its bouillabaisse, a tasty fish stew.

- The cathedral at Chartres is famous for its thirteenth-century stained glass windows. A masterpiece of Gothic architecture, it took less than thirty years to build in the mid-1300s.

- Bergerac is located in the Aquitaine region in southwestern France. Cyrano de Bergerac, a French satirist and dramatist, was a famous literary figure in the mid-1600s. He has been portrayed in many romantic legends, the most famous of which is Edmond Rostand's play *Cyrano de Bergerac*, in which he is shown as a tender, sentimental gallant with a horribly large nose.

- Avignon is a city in southeastern France. It is famous, among other things, for its Saint-Bénézet bridge, which crosses the Rhône River. The bridge was built between 1177 and 1188, and four of its arches still reach out toward the town.

- Saint-Tropez is a famous French resort on the Mediterranean.

- Provence was a former province in southeastern France, surrounding the modern-day area of Provence-Alpes-Côte d'Azur. It was founded by the Greeks but taken over by the Romans, becoming the first Roman province outside of Italy.

- The French spend francs to buy copies of *Le Monde* (*The World*), the French newspaper that is considered one of the best in "le monde."

- A famous sculpture of a man bent over from the waist with his head in his hand (called the *Thinker*) is just one of many sculptures by the master Auguste Rodin. It is in the Musée Rodin in Paris.

- The Seine is the second-longest river in France after the Loire.

- The term "eau de Paris" refers jokingly to the characteristic strong scent in the air of Paris.

GERMANY

Willkommen to the Federal Republic of Germany! Home of Oktoberfest, schnitzel, dachshunds, hofbrau, strudel, good beers, cuckoo clocks, and bratwurst, Germany (Deutschland in German) is found in central Europe.

Germany is a country of varied landscapes. There are mountains in the southern part (including the Bavarian Alps), hills and plateaus in the central area, and plains in the north. The northern plains are marked by many marshes and lakes. Germany also breaks up into a few islands in the North Sea near the Danish border.

The southern areas of Germany have dense forests. The Bohemian Forest is found in the southeastern corner of the country, near the border of the Czech Republic. The Black Forest was so-named because the trees used to grow so thick and so close together that it was actually dark in the forest. It is located in the southwestern corner of the country, near France. The Danube River, the second-longest river in Europe, rises there. Other major German rivers are the Elbe, the Rhine, the Oder, and the Weser.

Germany is a major industrial nation, known for iron and steel production, chemicals, precision engineering tools, and, of course, cars from companies like Mercedes-Benz, BMW, and Volkswagen.

Historically, Germany was composed of many different tribes who shared the same language. They fought with the Romans and were part of Charlemagne's Frankish empire. During the Thirty Years' War from 1618 to 1648, Germany was split into small areas and kingdoms. It wasn't really unified until Otto von Bismarck, a Prussian, formed the North German Confederation out of all those independent states in 1867. Three years later Germany went to war with its neighbor, France. After the defeat of France, Bismarck formed the German Empire and appointed King Wilhelm I of Prussia to be the German emperor (or kaiser).

In the twentieth century Germany was an aggressive force in two major wars—the First and Second World Wars. Kaiser Wilhelm was defeated in the First World War by the united forces of France, England, the United States, and other Allies. From 1919 to 1933 Germany was a republic under the Weimar constitution and had two presidents. The country was paying off debts and making reparations for the war when it was affected severely by the Great Depression. The times were so harsh—and the money was so worthless—that there are actually stories of people wheeling wheelbarrows full of money to stores to buy a loaf of bread, only to have the wheelbarrow stolen—not the money.

Adolf Hitler led the Nazi party and was appointed chancellor of

Germany in 1933. In 1934 he was named the fuehrer (leader). Hitler established the totalitarian Third Reich and became dictator of Germany. He made laws that curtailed Germans' freedom of speech and other basic civil rights. He then began a frightening program of Jewish persecution. Outside of Germany, Hitler's armies invaded the Sudetenland, an area between Germany and Czechoslovakia, and then Austria, which was declared German. When Germany invaded Poland in 1939, the Second World War began. Hitler made an alliance with Japan and Italy, and together with other countries these nations (called the Axis Powers) fought the combined forces of the Soviet Union, England, France, the United States (called the "Big Four," or the Allied Powers), and other allies. During the war, Hitler set up brutal concentration camps where millions of Jews, Gypsies, political opponents, and others were systematically murdered in what was called the Holocaust. There is a Holocaust museum at Dachau, one of the more infamous camps. When it was clear that Germany was defeated in the war, Hitler committed suicide in Berlin in 1945.

Germany gave up a considerable amount of land at the end of the war to the Soviet Union and Poland. In an effort to weaken Germany so that it would never be able to mount a war machine again, the country was divided by occupying forces. East Germany was administered by the Soviets. The capital city of Berlin was divided into four parts, each controlled by one of the major Allied Powers.

The eastern part of Germany wasn't as industrialized as the western part, and millions of immigrants fled the Soviet domination of the area until 1961, when the Berlin Wall was built, dividing the city and the country into two distinct parts. This wall separated East Germany from the more democratic West

Germany and stood as a symbol of division until it was torn down. Germany was reunified in October of 1990 and is now one country again.

Germany today is a richly diverse country. Different regions have different identities and customs. In the southern regions like Bavaria, there are annual beer festivals. People wear traditional costumes, sing and dance, and drink beer. There are also many famous castles in the Bavarian Alps, like Neuchwanstein, Linderhof, and Hohenschwangau. There are also castles along the banks of the Rhine River, in the western part of the country.

The autobahn is the famous expressway system that goes through Germany. Although in the past the autobahn had no speed limits at all, it is now regulated.

Other Facts About Germany

- Germans spend marks when they buy wood carvings and other folk arts from the Black Forest.

- Heidelberg is the site of the oldest university in Europe.

- The city of Bonn is known for its baroque architecture, and as the birthplace of Ludwig van Beethoven, the legendary composer.

- Other famous German composers have included Johann Sebastian Bach, Richard Wagner, and Hildegard von Bingen.

- Köln, or Cologne, is the fourth-largest city in Germany. It is the historic, cultural, and economic capital of the Rhineland. Its cathedral is the largest Gothic church in northern Europe.

- Munich, the third-largest city in Germany, is the capital of the state of Bavaria. Henry the Lion founded the city in the year 1157.

- Dresden was called "the Florence on the Elbe" before the Second

World War. It was considered to be one of the world's most beautiful cities because of its architecture and art treasures. Dresden was nearly destroyed by bombings during the war. Some of its buildings have been restored, including Zwinger Palace, a museum known for its exquisite porcelain sculptures.

- Dresden was also famed for its opera. Carl Maria von Weber and Richard Wagner conducted in the Opera House, and operas by Richard Strauss were first performed there.

- Hannover is known as the "garden city" for its beautiful parks, public gardens, and woods.

- Brandenburg is famous for its beautiful cathedrals. Johann Sebastian Bach composed six beautiful concertos called the Brandenburg Concertos.

- Look out for hot water in Baden-Baden! The city is a spa and still has Roman baths.

- Leipzeig, the birthplace of baroque composer Johann Sebastian Bach, was part of East Germany until the reunification of Germany.

- International trade fairs have been held in the city of Frankfurt since the year 1240. Not too surprisingly, Frankfurt is the site from which the Rothschild family started its international banking empire.

- Jacob and Wilhelm Grimm, from the Hesse district, told marvelous folktales from their native Germany that have become some of the most popular stories in the world. Known as the Brothers Grimm, they gave us *Hansel and Gretel,* among many other tales.

- Bremen, on the Weser River, is one of the most important port cities in Germany.

- Dortmund was originally called Throtmanni in the year 885. There are four moated castles there.

- The city of Hamburg, on the Elbe River, is the second-most populous city in Germany.

- Düsseldorf is on the Rhine. The existence of Neanderthal man was first discovered in the nearby Neanderthal valley. The remains, estimated to be between 30,000 and 250,000 years old, were discovered in the Feldhofer Cave in 1856.

- Bingen is a port city where the Rhine and the Nahe rivers meet. It originated as the Roman fortress of Bingium. Bingen is famous for the "Mouse Tower" or the Mauseturm, a rock in the Rhine. Saxon folk legend has it that in 973, the Archbishop Hatto I of Mainz was gnawed to death by mice on the rock in punishment for wrongdoing.

- The city of Essen is the industrial hub of the Ruhr. It was a center of Germany's war industry during the Second World War and suffered heavy destruction during that time.

- Albert Einstein, the famous physicist, was born in Ulm, Germany.

- German playwright and poet Bertolt Brecht revolutionized theater and drama. He wrote *The Threepenny Opera*, among many other plays.

- Checkpoint Charlie, on the Friedrichstrasse, was one of most famous parts of the Berlin Wall, where soldiers were stationed to prevent people from crossing between East and West Berlin.

GREECE

When you think of Greece, you have to think about the sea. Set on the southern tip of the Balkan Peninsula, Greece is surrounded by ocean and includes around 2,000 islands in its territory. The largest island is Crete, but there are many more in the Mediterranean, Ionian, and Aegean seas that surround the small peninsula that is attached to the rest of Europe.

Historically, Greece is considered to be the "cradle of Western civilization." From its rich mythology and pantheon of gods like Zeus, Hermes, Hera, and Aphrodite, to its philosophers, scientists, writers, and poets, Greece has left its mark on history. Among the names we remember today are Euripides, the father of modern tragedy; Aesop, whose fables are told to this day; Aristophanes, whose comic plays like *The Clouds* are a permanent part of the literature of the theater; Archimedes, whose scientific discoveries were among the most advanced of his time; Pythagorus, for whom the Pythagorean theorem of geometry was named; Socrates, Plato, Homer, Plutarch. . . . It is safe to say that our lives today were profoundly influenced by these people who lived hundreds of years before the birth of Christ.

Greek inventions and innovations still exist today, or have been revived. The Olympics started in Greece, as did the running marathon (named after the city of Marathon). Gymnastics, the javelin, and the discus are all sports that have roots in ancient Greece.

The Greeks were the first civilization to use democracy as a form of government. In fact the word democracy means rule of the people (from *demos*, "people," and *kratos*, "rule"). After the fall of the Greeks, it was nearly 2,000 years before our modern form of democracy became established.

Athens is the capital of Greece, and has been so for centuries. The jewel in Athens's crown is the Parthenon, a temple originally built for the goddess Athena, for whom Athens was named. Built on a 500-foot hill called the Acropolis, the Parthenon is a great example of ancient Greek architecture and, according to some, a marvel of simplicity and design.

Other Facts About Greece

- The study of rhetoric was developed in Greece and Rome. Aristotle called it "the art of persuasion."

- One of Aristotle's concepts was called the Golden Mean, which was a sort of middle path between extremes, similar to the "middle path" of the Buddha.

- Magnificent examples of ancient Greek sculpture still exist today, often depicting gods like Zeus and Athena.

- The Peloponnese (or Peloponncsus) is a large peninsula that is attached to the rest of Greece by a very narrow strip of land called the Isthmus of Corinth. The ancient city of Sparta is located on the Peloponnese.

- The Pindus Mountains run vertically through the center of the Greek mainland.

- Mount Olympus was the mythical home of Zeus and the other Greek gods. However, there is a real Mount Olympus in the northwest of Greece. It is the highest place in Greece, at 9,570 feet.

- Founded in 316 B.C., Thessaloniki was named after one of the sisters of Alexander the Great of Macedonia. Thessaloniki was at one time the capital of Macedonia.

- Levkas is both the name of one of the Greek isles and the name of the main city found on that island.

- The city of Sparta was once one of the most powerful of the Greek city-states. Spartans were dedicated to a severe warlike life, from which we get the adjective "spartan," which refers to someone who lives very simply and without luxury.

- The city of Olympia is thought to be the original site of the Olympic games as long ago as 776 B.C.

- Ithaca is the second smallest of the major Greek islands. Paxos is the smallest.

- Legend has it that the island of Mykonos (or Mikonos) was the rock thrown by Heracles to defeat the Giants. Mykonos means "white island."

- At one time, the temple at Delphi was considered to be the center of the world. (Delphi is an ancient site, probably inhabited since the fourteenth century B.C.) At the foot of Mt. Parnassus, this was where, according to legend, the earth goddess Gaea ruled over the Oracle of Delphi, which was guarded by the serpent Python. Later, the legend says, the god Apollo killed Python and set up his own oracle there.

- Knossos is an ancient city on the island of Crete. It is thought to be the ancient capital of the legendary king Minos. As part of the legend, the feared Minotaur, with the head of a bull on the body of a man, was imprisoned in a great labyrinth. King Minos ordered sacrifices to the Minotaur until the legendary hero Theseus went into the labyrinth and slew the monster.

- Samos was the birthplace of the philosopher and mathematician Pythagoras, and one of the places where ancient Greek sculpture flourished.

- Rhodes is both the name of one of the Greek islands and the name of the principal city on that island. One of the historical landmarks of Rhodes was the Colossus of Rhodes, one of the Seven Wonders of the Ancient World. Standing more than 100 feet high and made of bronze, it was toppled in an earthquake in about 225 B.C.; 878 years later, it was dismantled by Arabic raiders and carried away in pieces on 900 camels.

- Achilles was a legendary fighter whose mother dipped him in the River Styx to make him invulnerable to attack. She didn't dip his heel, however, because she held him by it, and this was his downfall. This is where we get the expression "Achilles heel," which means a person's particular weakness.

- Olives and olive oil are among the special foods of Greece. In particular, the kalamata olive is prized.

- Feta cheese is a soft, white, salty cheese made from the milk of goats.

- Moussaka is similar to lasagne, but made with layers of eggplant, ground meat, and other ingredients.

- Baklava is a traditional dessert made from thin sheets of phyllo pastry with honey and pistachios or other nuts.

- In today's Olympic games, the lit Olympic torch is carried by a series of runners who start in Greece and end at the site of the games, wherever they are in the world. The runners do not let the torch's flame go out.

- Homer wrote both the *Iliad* and the *Odyssey*, but little is known about him. The *Iliad* is about a war between Troy (also known as Ilias) and a confederation of Greek armies. The *Odyssey* is about the adventures of Odysseus (also known as Ulysses), a Greek king on his way home from the Trojan War.

GUATEMALA

The Mayans flourished in Guatemala for more than 3,000 years, building great temples by hand without the help of pack animals or the wheel. But their civilization faded, and by the time the Spanish explorer Pedro Alvarado arrived there around 1524, the Mayans were easily conquered. Antigua Guatemala, the ancient Spanish capital, was destroyed by an earthquake in 1773, and the capital was moved to Guatemala City. You might say that Guatemala is tectonically challenged, or earthquake prone. The most recent great earthquake occured in 1976; it devastated large areas of the country.

Guatemala is basically an agricultural state that occupies a section of Central America between the Pacific Ocean and the Caribbean Sea. Among the crops grown in Guatemala are coffee (the leading crop), chicle (the chewy part of chewing gum), mahogany, sugar, cotton, rubber, cardamom, and bananas. Once, much of the land was owned by the United Fruit Company (a U.S. company), which exported fruits mainly to the United States. Because the economy of the country relied so heavily on this single business, Guatemala was once derogatorily called a "banana republic."

Like many Central and South American countries, Guatemala was ruled by a series of dictatorships, and politics in the country have been unstable for most of the twentieth century. In 1986 Guatemala adopted a constitutional government with free elections.

While Spanish is the official language of the country, more than twenty Indian languages are still spoken, and the country is largely comprised of Indians and Ladinos (people of mixed Spanish and Indian ancestry). The Indians of Guatemala have retained their original lifestyles and have largely avoided adopting European ways. The fact that they have been ruled for most of this century by a series of dictatorships and that wealth is unevenly distributed in the country may account for their lack of Westernization.

Other Facts About Guatemala

- The national bird, the quetzal, was so prized for its radiant feathers that now there are few left. The monetary unit of Guatemala is also called the quetzal.

- Even though the Mayans lacked pack animals and the wheel, their astronomer priests were quite advanced in some ways. For instance, their calendar was more accurate than the old European calendar.

- The Mayan ruins at Tikal are located in the area called the Petén. At its height, around A.D. 700, Tikal was thought to have housed about 10,000 people, with about 50,000 more living in the vicinity. Today, the ruins provide excellent examples of Mayan temples, hieroglyphics, and other artifacts.

- The Petén is a low-lying plateau that constitutes about one third of the territory of Guatemala. Most of the land is covered by heavy tropical rain forests.

- El Mirador is another ancient Mayan ruin that was discovered in the extreme northern part of Petén in the twentieth century.

- Quezaltenango was destroyed by the Santa Maria volcano in 1902, but it is now Guatemala's second-largest city.

- Jalapa is the name of a city and also of a region (called a departmento, or department) of Guatemala. It is quite isolated and still retains much of the original Spanish colonial architecture of its past.

- Flores (which means "flowers" in Spanish) was once the capital of the Itzá Indians, a Mayan tribe who successfully resisted the Spanish conquerors for more than 150 years. Now it is the capital of the departmento of Petén. It is built on San Adreas Island in the southern part of Lake Petén.

- First established in 1538, the city of Cobán was once a major commercial and manufacturing center, but with the opening of a new highway in 1958, much of its business has shifted to Guatemala City. Near Cobán is a 250-mile system of caves and underground grottoes (man-made caves) called the Lanquín Caves.

- Until the 1970s Puerto Barrios was Guatemala's main port. It is built on Amatique Bay in the Gulf of Honduras. However, because Puerto Barrios was controlled largely by foreign interests, the Guatemalan government constructed a government-owned port at Santo Tomás de Castillia six miles south.

- The Tajumulco volcano, also know as Mount Tajumulco, is the highest peak in Central America, at 13,845 feet.

- Lake Atitlán was formed by the activities of nearby volcanoes, and three cone-shaped volcanoes surround it. They are called Atitlán, Tolimán, and San Pedro.

- Lake Izabal drains through the Dulce River into Amatique Bay. The principal settlement on its shores is called El Estor, which was originally a trading outpost for the United Fruit Company. Its name is taken from the English word "store."

- The Motagua River is approximately 250 miles long, making it Guatemala's longest river.

- Throughout Latin America, the Day of the Dead (Día de los Muertos) is a popular and colorful ceremony. It is said that the souls of the dead return every year on October 31 and November 1.

- In 1823, Guatemala joined Honduras, El Salvador, Costa Rica, and Nicaragua to form the United Provinces of Central America. The region was racked by nearly constant political upheaval, however, and by 1840 the United Provinces were no longer united.

HUNGARY

Where in the world would you eat chicken paprikás off fine porcelain before dancing a czardas? Only in Hungary! Hungary is a unique country in Eastern Europe. Its people are descendants of nomadic tribes called the Magyars, and they speak a language called Magyar, or Hungarian. Hungarian is not related to any Slavic languages, although most of Hungary's neighbors, such as Slovenia, the former Yugoslavia, Ukraine, Croatia, and Slovakia, are Slavic-speaking countries.

The country itself is a large, flat plain, among the most fertile farmland in Europe. The larger part of the plain is called the Great Alfold, while the hillier Little Alfold is found in the north-west area of the country. The plains are also called the puszta. The Danube and the Tisza rivers cut across them. The Danube runs along the Slovakian border, and turns south just north of Budapest. The Körös River joins the Tisza in the southwest corner of the country.

Hungary is famous for its beautiful Lake Balaton, the largest lake in central Europe. This lake covers 230 square miles, and is the source of much tourism in Hungary. Tourists also enjoy the hot thermal springs in Hungary. The Romans brought the concept of baths built around hot springs to Eastern Europe. Hungary has 154 hot-spring baths open to the public, including the famous Gellert Baths in Budapest.

Budapest, the capital city, was originally two separate towns on opposite sides of the Danube River. Buda, on the right bank, and Pest, on the left, were united into one city. Castle Hill, in Buda, is a famous and beautiful place overlooking the Danube. Budapest is famous for its stunning architecture, like the parliament building, the State Opera House, and the National Theater. The Hungarian National Museum is also found in Budapest. St. Stephen's crown, the symbol of Hungarian nation-hood, can be seen there. Many of the historic buildings have had to undergo massive restorations since being damaged during the Second World War.

Early settlers in Hungary—Slavs and Germanic people—were taken over in the 800s by the Magyars. The Magyars were a herding people who knew how to fight fiercely. Steven I, also known as St. Steven, was the first king of Hungary. He ruled from the year 1000. Hungary was invaded many times by the Turks between the fifteenth and seventeenth centuries. The Turks were in Hungary for so long that today the Turkish and Hungarian languages have many words in common.

After the Turks were expelled, toward the end of the 1600s, Austria controlled Hungary. The Hungarians managed to keep their independence for the most part, even though they were ruled by the Austrian emperor. Finally, the two merged to become the Austro-Hungarian Empire, and the emperor of Austria was also the king of Hungary. Austria-Hungary was one of the most powerful empires in Europe until its defeat in the First World War in 1918. A lot of the land that had been Austria-Hungary was given to Romania, Czechoslovakia, and Yugoslavia. All of these countries already had large Hungarian populations.

Hungary fought with Germany during the Second World War, and was occupied by the Soviet Union at the end of the war. Hungary declared itself an independent republic in 1946 and later attempted to overthrow the communist government in the famous 1956 revolution. The Soviets responded by invading Budapest. Over 200,000 people fled the country as the communists seized power again. Over thirty years later, Hungary was one of the first Eastern European countries to establish a non-communist government. Soviet troops didn't actually leave Hungary until 1991.

Hungary industrialized rapidly after the Second World War. It is known for steel and iron production, as well as the manufacture of buses. Nearly one fifth of the workforce in Hungary, however, is in agriculture.

Today, Hungary is a popular tourist attraction. Millions of people travel each year to visit the city where Buda meets Pest, to sample Hungarian goulash, and to listen to the haunting violins of Gypsy and other folk musicians.

Other Facts About Hungary

- The southern city of Szeged is known for the fine paprika that is made there. Paprika is a spice made from sweet red peppers, and it is the main reason why Hungarian cuisine is so unique.

- When Hungarians buy their wonderful wines, they pay for them in forints.

- Ernö Rubik, inventor of the Rubik's Cube, is Hungarian.

- Béla Bartók, Franz Liszt, and Zoltán Kodály are among the famous musical composers to come from Hungary.

- Debrecen is the home of Hungary's oldest printing press, which has been operating since 1561.

- Pecs had the earliest university in Hungary, founded in 1367. It was abolished by the Turks but reopened in 1922. It is also a city known for its production of ceramic ware.

- Gyor is a historic town known for its old architecture and river channels from the Marcal and the Raba that meander through the city. It is also where many bus parts—like frames—are made.

- Koszeg, a border town near Austria, is known for its old buildings, churches, and medieval fortress.

- Attila Jozsef was one of the greatest poets of the twentieth century. His poems were first published when he was seventeen years old. He died at the young age of thirty-two.

- King Steven I was born in the town of Esztergom and was crowned king there in 1000.

- Esterhazy Palace, one of the great sights of Hungary, is in the town of Fertod. It was called "the Hungarian Versailles" and was completed in 1766.

- The town of Sopron was settled by many different peoples, including the Celts, before it was occupied by the Romans.

- The second major industrial town after Budapest, Miskolc is known for production of cement, glass, and textiles. Wine making is important, too, and the limestone caves in Avas are used as cellars!

- In the mid-1400s, King Mathias Corvinus was the only national king to reign over all Hungary after the Arpads were gone. He was a Renaissance prince who welcomed artists and scholars to his court.

- In Hungary's Heroes Square there is a monument that commemorates the settling of Hungary and the history of the Hungarian people.

ICELAND

Variously called "The Land of Lava and Ice" or "The Island of the Midnight Sun," Iceland is definitely a country of extremes. With approximately 100 volcanoes and hot springs in about 250 locations, you could easily say that Iceland contradicts its name. Located just below the Arctic Circle, Iceland is certainly pretty cold. Just south of the Greenland Sea and west of the Norwegian Sea, it is a land of giant icebergs and Arctic winds, but Iceland's weather is surprisingly mild for a country so far to the north. That's because warm water from the Gulf Stream keeps temperatures just a little toastier than you'd expect.

Although very little of the land can be farmed, about one fifth of Iceland is good grazing land, and a wool industry has developed there. Fishing accounts for about one sixth of the economy of Iceland, with cod and herring the predominant catch. Manufacturing makes up only about one tenth of the total economy. Major products include aluminum, ferrosilicon, diatomite, and textiles.

Because of its great water and geothermal wealth (the heat from all those volcanoes and hot springs), Iceland is able to supply warmth to homes and to the many greenhouses where vegetables are cultivated by harnessing the heat directly available from the earth. Iceland's electricity is supplied by hydroelectric power.

Politically, Iceland's Althing is the oldest existing parliament in the world, dating back nearly 1,100 years. Its roots go back to the time of the Vikings, who first settled the area in the ninth century. Vikings passed through Iceland, settling there and continuing on westward to Greenland and even to the Americas. The famous Norwegian Viking Erik the Red is said to have passed through Iceland on his way to colonize Greenland. And it was Erik's son, Leif Eriksson, who is credited in the ancient Icelandic sagas with being the first European to reach the Americas.

The Vikings believed in the old Norse legends and the gods such as Odin, Loki, and Thor, and these legends accompanied them to Iceland. However, in the tenth century, the Althing passed a law that all Icelanders would henceforth be Christians.

But the old traditions didn't die altogether. Icelanders are great storytellers, with a long literary tradition. Skalds, or poet/singers, wrote many verses between the ninth and thirteenth centuries. One of the great masterpieces of Scandinavian literature, the *Elder Edda*, is a later work that is considered to be a different poetic form from the skaldic poetry. But the stories of the Icelandic writers give us a history of Viking heroes, Norse gods, and great events in the history of the region. Their writing tradition continued into this century, as Icelander Halldór Laxness won the Nobel Prize for literature in 1955.

Other Facts About Iceland

- The Icelandic language is descended from Old Norse. Norse was once spoken from Labrador to the north of Germany; now it is spoken only in Iceland.

- Although it has remained essentially an independent republic, Iceland has been under the control of both Norway and Denmark during its long history.

- Statistically, Iceland has the highest life expectancy in the world.

- Vigdis Finnbogadottir was the first woman to become the head of a country by democratic election.

- Iceland must be a friendly place. Its telephone books are alphabetized by first name instead of by last name.

- Iceland is the farthest west of the Scandinavian countries.

- Iceland is known for its great fishing and for its abundant bird life. A colony of ducks at Lake Myvatn is the largest such colony in the world. It is the home of many puffins and penguins as well.

- Reykjavík, the capital of Iceland and the northernmost capital in the world, literally means "bay of smokes."

- The word geyser comes from Geysír, the great geyser, located in Árnes, which has been spouting boiling water since at least the thirteenth century. Although it doesn't spout as often today, possibly because of debris thrown into it by careless people, it still can send plumes of water up to 200 feet in the air.

- When you visit Iceland, you will need to exchange your dollars for kronur.

- The city of Akureyri is one of the economic centers of northern Iceland.

- You might not find the city of Straumsvik on many maps.

- The volcano called Mount Hekla has also been known as the

Mountain of Hell. It has erupted fourteen times since 1104, the last time in 1970.

- Detti Falls (or Dettifoss) is Iceland's largest waterfall. Its vertical drop is 144 feet, and it is a great source of natural beauty and hydroelectric power.

- The Shetland Islands, where Shetland ponies first came from, are southwest of Iceland.

- After the Second World War, Iceland extended its fishing limits from three miles offshore to 200 miles in an effort to protect its fishing resources. For years, the British protested this policy and sent out naval vessels to protect British fishing boats. This disagreement, not really a war, was dubbed the "cod wars." In 1976 the British acknowledged Iceland's claims and the cod wars came to an end.

- Note: In case you didn't figure it out, the clue that mentions "frozen water" is referring to "ice."

INDIA

Holy cow! There's one country in the world where cows are considered sacred, where you'd spend rupees to buy a bowl of curry with some chutney on the side and perhaps take a ride on an elephant. If you're guessing that it's India, you're right.

India, the seventh-largest country in the world, is the second-most populous country. There are more than 900 million people in India! Although it is technically on the continent of Asia, it occupies nearly all of a huge peninsula called the Indian sub-continent. The peninsula lies between the Bay of Bengal, the Indian Sea, and the Arabian Sea.

India, or Bharat in Hindi, is made up of varied landscapes including broad plains, tropical lowlands, jungles, and the Thar Desert. Along the northern borders run the Himalaya Mountains. The Ganges River rises in the Himalayas and runs along the northern parts of India.

India has three basic seasons: cool, hot, and rainy. The monsoons sweep in from June to September, during which time the country receives most of its rainfall.

India has one of the oldest civilizations in the world. The development of India throughout history is a story of many invaders and conquerers. The Indus Valley civilization started in 2500 B.C. Aryan invaders arrived from the north around the year 1500 B.C. and apparently brought Hinduism with them. Hinduism is the major religion in India today. The Aryans spoke Sanskrit, the language in which many of the early Indian sacred writings were composed. India today has hundreds of different languages and Sanskrit has died out, but most people speak English as a common tongue.

Buddhism, too, spread rapidly during the 200s B.C. The Mauryas and the Guptas made India a center of art and learning. Much later, European traders and invaders began arriving, beginning with the Portuguese in A.D. 1498. The Islamic Mughals conquered India in the 1500s. The Mughals ruled until 1857. The British set up the East India Trading Company and gained control of most of India officially in 1858.

After the First World War, there was much unrest in India and a great deal of resentment toward British rule. Mohandas Gandhi, or Mahatma ("Great Soul") as he was called, was an Indian lawyer who became a leader against the British. He began a program of nonviolent resistance to English control. It was successful because the Indians refused to buy English goods or to cooperate with the English laws. Gandhi himself was assassinated by a disgruntled Hindu in January of 1948.

India became independent in 1947. It was a democratic republic as of 1950, and today it is the world's largest democracy.

Shortly after independence, two regions of northern India dominated by Muslims broke away from Hindu India and established the state of Pakistan. Since 1947, India and Pakistan have fought sporadically over a region called Kashmir.

India has long been one of the centers of spiritual and religious thought and philosophy in the world. The *Bhagavad Gita*, "The Song of God," is one the greatest and most beautiful of Hindu scriptures. It is part of Book VI of the *Mahabharata*, an epic poem. In the *Bhagavad Gita*, the warrior prince Arjuna converses with his friend Krishna, who is really the god Vishnu.

During the Vedic period of India, Brahma was one of the major gods of Hinduism, a kind of creator. Eventually Brahma lost importance to the gods Vishnu and Shiva. The three form the major triad of Hinduism. Vishnu was worshipped as the protector and preserver of the world. He was also the restorer of dharma (moral order). Vishnu was said to appear through the forms of Rama and Krishna. He rode the bird Garuda. Shiva is the most complex of the Hindu gods, both destroyer and creator. According to legend, he brought the Ganges River to Earth. He allowed the water to flow through his hair so it wouldn't fall to Earth too hard.

Other Facts About India

- The country of India during British rule was immortalized by author Rudyard Kipling. He is known for *The Jungle Book, Just So Stories*, and other children's books, as well as more serious, thought-provoking tales of British soldiers in India.

- New Delhi is the capital of India. It was built between 1912 and 1929, and replaced the old capital, Calcutta.

- Bombay is the financial and commercial center of India. It is one of the largest, most densely populated cities in the world. The city itself occupies a group of former islands. It is incredibly poverty-stricken and has the largest slums in India.

- One third of the population of Calcutta lives in slums. It was the capital of British India from 1772 to 1912.

- Nagpur is located on the Nag River, and is almost exactly in the middle of the country. The region is famous throughout the world for its oranges.

- Patna is a city that stretches along the Ganges River for about twelve miles. One of its landmarks is a Sikh temple.

- Agra was the capital of the Mughal Empire during some periods. Agra is best known as the site of the Taj Mahal. The Taj Mahal was built as a burial place for the wife of a Mughal emperor. Construction began in 1632 and wasn't finished until about 1643. It is one of the most beautiful buildings in the world.

- Darjeeling, whose name means "Place of the Thunderbolt," is known for its wonderful tea. It is about 7,000 feet high, on a ridge of the Sikkim Himalayas. On a clear day Mount Everest can be seen from Darjeeling.

- Sikhism is a religion that combines Muslim and Hindu elements. The Sikhs were originally a nonviolent sect, but they have become increasingly political and violent over the centuries.

- The Punjab region of India is the only Indian state that has a majority of Sikhs. The Golden Temple at Amritsar is the chief temple of the Sikhs. The Punjabi language is widely spoken.

- Cashmere goats come from Kashmir, and provide some of the softest animal-hair fiber in the world. Cashmere sweaters are greatly valued throughout the world.

- India was once ruled by maharajahs and maharanis. These were the Hindu words for rulers of one of the states of India. Maharajahs were male, and maharanis female, like kings and queens.

INDONESIA

It's the country of islands, 13,670 in all. Its capital is Jakarta, located on the island of Sumatra. Among its main territories are Java, Bali, Celebese, Brunei, Lombok, the Molucca Islands, and parts of Borneo (Kilimantan) and New Guinea (Irian Jaya). In addition to being the world's largest archipelago and the world's most populous island nation, Indonesia is the world's most populous Islamic nation, which may seem surprising since Islam began in the Middle East. Actually, many religions flourish in Indonesia, including Islam, Hinduism, Buddhism, and Christianity.

Historically, the Indonesian islands were populated by immigrants from mainland Asia. These are the ancestors of much of the Indonesian population of today. Over the centuries, traders from India and China brought culture and religion to the islands. During the sixteenth century, the Portuguese discovered the Molucca Islands, also known as the Spice Islands. They were followed by the Spaniards, the Dutch, and the British. The Dutch formed the Dutch East India Company and colonized the islands, forming the company's headquarters in a city called

Batavia, which is now called Jakarta. The Dutch remained in control, with only one break in the nineteenth century, until after the Second World War, when the leader of the Nationalist Party, Sukarno, declared independence from the Netherlands. Sukarno subsequently became president of the new United States of Indonesia.

When you ask "What's the good word?" in Indonesia, you never know what the answer will be. Based on the Malay language, Bahasa Indonesia is the national language of Indonesia. It incorporates words from Arabic, Portuguese, Chinese, Dutch, Spanish, and English.

Like Iceland far away to the north, Indonesia has a lot of active volcanoes—certainly more than 100, possibly as many as 220. One of the most famous volcanoes in the world is on an island in Indonesia. It is called Krakatoa, and in 1883 it erupted so violently, the explosion was heard half a world away.

Another interesting island is Komodo Island, where we get the name of the Komodo dragon, the largest lizard in the world. The Komodo dragon can reach up to ten feet long. They are found only on Komodo Island and a few islands nearby, but they are almost extinct due to overcollecting. Komodo dragons are among the world's many protected species.

Other animals found in Indonesia are from two separate groups, the Asian and the Australian. Examples of Asian animals found in Indonesia are the rhinoceros, orangutan, tapir, tiger, elephant, and water buffalo. Among the Australian animals found there are the cockatoo, bowerbird, and bird of paradise.

Although most of the islands are tropical rain forests, about a third of the land is considered suitable for agriculture. By far the most common crop is rice, and it is not unusual to see workers standing in rice paddies wearing sarongs with printed batik patterns. Other crops grown on the islands include spices like cloves and nutmeg, and various wood products, including rubber, which was once harvested on plantations owned by the Dutch. Coffee, tea, and tobacco are also grown in Indonesia. Indonesia is the world's leading source of tin, and it also produces petroleum and natural gas.

Indonesia is a culturally rich area famous for its arts and dance. The famous wayang kulit, or shadow-puppet theater, delights people of all ages. The music of the gamelan, an orchestra composed mostly of various sized gongs, is striking and unique, and dancers from Java and Bali are both colorful and exotic. In fact, dance in Java and Bali is a highly evolved art form. It is said that on Bali there is no separate word for art. Every person is engaged in the art of living, and they paint, play music, dance, sing, carve, and otherwise express themselves through art as they live.

Other Facts About Indonesia

- The Legong dance involves two preadolescent girls whose rapid movements are carried out in unison.

- If you're going to tip the becak driver, get out your rupiah before leaving the three-wheeled taxi.

- Enjoy the beef satay, and don't forget the peanut sauce. Then follow it with a fried rice dish surrounded by meats called nasi goreng and some curried vegetables.

- The world's largest Buddhist shrine is on the island of Java. It is called Borobudur, and it was constructed of 2,000,000 cubic feet of gray volcanic stone. Borobudur features several common Buddhist symbols, including the stupa (originally a relic mound), the mandala (a mystic symbol of the universe), and the mystic mountain. At the top of the shrine is a single stupa that towers 103 feet above the base.

- Bandung is a city in the interior of Java where Sundanese culture thrives. In 1955 it was the site of an important conference that denounced Western colonialism.

- The city of Palembang dates back at least to the seventh century. Located on the banks of the Musi River, it was once the capital of the Buddhist Shrivijaya Empire.

- Pakanbaru is the capital of the Sumatran province of Riau.

- Semarang is a major port city on the Semarang River on the island of Java.

- Medan is a port city on the island of Sumatra. It was once the home of the sultan of Deli, and it lies along the Deli River. Two universities are located in Medan—the University of North Sumatra and the Islamic University of North Sumatra.

- Surabaya is the second-largest city in Indonesia, after Jakarta. Surabaya is a port city that has been the center of much fighting both during the Second World War and in the struggle for independence that followed. It is located across the Surabaya Strait from Madura Island. The Mas River flows through the center of the city.

- Not surprisingly, the Molucca Islands are located in the Molucca Sea.

- There are many other seas among the Indonesian Islands, including the Flores Sea, the Celebese Sea, the Java Sea, and the Banda Sea. To the north are the South China Sea and the Pacific Ocean. To the south is the Indian Ocean.

- The Sunda Shelf is a vast, shallow area of ocean, 690,000 square miles, that was once above sea level. Many of the Indonesian islands are parts of the shelf that remain above water. The Lesser Sunda Islands are among the many volcanically active islands on the shelf.

- Kampong is the Malay word for town.

- Hari Raya is a very important Islamic holiday celebrated in Indonesia.

- A mandi is a bathtub.

- Malang is best known for its production of fruits, vegetables, and flowers.

- In Malay, pasar means marketplace or bazaar.

- The island of Bangka is one of the chief tin producing centers in the world. It is located east of Sumatra, across the Strait of Bangka.

- Sinkep is one of the Indonesian islands that has tin mines.

- The skull of Java Man was discovered in 1891 at Trinil, near the Solo River. It has been determined to be the skull of a pre-human species called *Pithecanthus erectus*. Java Man was thought to have lived at least 700,000 years ago.

- Mata Hari was a famous dancer and spy who lived part of her life in Java. The name Mata Hari means literally "eye of the day"—in other words, the sun.

- A sarong is a four- or five-yard piece of rectangular fabric that is wrapped around the body to form a dress or skirt. Sarongs are worn by both men and women and can be wrapped in a variety of ways. The most prized sarongs are woven with gold thread and come from Batu Bara and Sumatra.

- Batik is a process of dyeing that uses wax to prevent the dye from absorbing in certain places, thereby allowing the creation of complex patterns and designs on the cloth. Between dyeings, the cloth is boiled to remove the wax; then wax is reapplied as necessary. Batik can be used on surfaces other than cloth. For instance, on Celebese Island the wax is applied to bamboo strips.

IRAN

C an you think of an Islamic country that was the birthplace of the famous poet Omar Khayyám? A country just south of the Caspian Sea? Where shahs used to rule but now ayatollahs do? It's on the Persian Gulf but isn't called Persia anymore. It's the Islamic Republic of Iran.

Iran is a mostly mountainous country with a central plateau that has two deserts in it. The Dasht-e-Kavir ("Great Salt Desert") and the Dasht-e-Lut ("Great Sand Desert") occupy about half of Iran's land. They are ringed by mountain ranges, including the high Elburz Mountains as well as the Zagros and the Bashakerd Mountains. Mount Demavend, the highest mountain in Iran, is in the Elburz range and rises to 18,396 feet.

The only really fertile areas in Iran lie near the Caspian Sea and in some mountain foothills. Iran also has salt lakes, rivers like the Karun River, and other lakes. Lake Urmia, the largest of the lakes in Iran, is near the border Iran shares with Turkey and Iraq.

Iran was the center of the Persian Empire. The Persians came to the region in the second millenium B.C., from the east. They were an Indo-European people who were related to the Aryans of India. In 549 B.C. the empire was united as the Medes, and the Persians joined together under Cyrus the Great. There are famous ruins near Shiraz of Persepolis, which was the capital of Persia under Darius the Great. The city's construction was begun after the death of Cyrus. Persia was overrun by the Greeks and the Parthians, but the Persians maintained their independence. In the seventh century A.D., Arabs invaded and brought Islam with them.

Persia from the ninth century was a major cultural and artistic center of the world. Later, it was ruled by Turks and Mongols until the sixteenth century. In the 1800s, Russia and England both tried to gain control of Iran. Afghanistan was severed from Iran by the British in 1857.

Once oil was discovered in the region, the British and the Americans and other western powers wanted to maintain influence in Iran. Dictatorlike shahs were put into power. Reza Pahlavi, who became shah in 1941, modernized Iran but was a despot in many ways. The last shah was deposed in 1979, when Iran underwent a revolution. An Islamic government was put into power, with the Ayatollah Khomeini as its head.

Under the ayatollahs, Iran has been ruled by fundamentalist Islamic clerics. Strict laws are followed according to the Koran, the holy book of Islam. The people of Iran are mostly Shi'ite Muslims, a minority of Muslims worldwide. Most Muslims, including the majority of Arabs, are Sunni. The Shi'a are much stricter about the way the laws are followed and interpreted than the Sunnis.

The Five Pillars of Islam, the practices that every devout Muslim is supposed to follow, are: the profession of faith, prayer five times a day, the giving of alms for the poor, fasting during the month of Ramadan (a holy season), and the hajj, or pilgrimage to Mecca, a city in Saudi Arabia. In Iran, as in most Islamic countries, many women wear a black veil that conceals most of their faces. The veil is called a chador.

Since Iran has been Islamic for so long, the country has many fine examples of Islamic architecture and art. Mosques (temples), like the Blue Mosque in Tabriz and the Masjid-i-Shah Cheragh, are known for their beautiful decor. The Blue Mosque is so called because it is decorated in blue tiles. The Shah Cheragh shrine was built from 1344 to 1349, in Shiraz. In many Iranian cities, minarets mix with modern buildings, and the haunting voices of the muezzins (criers) can be heard calling the faithful to prayer. A minaret is a tower that is connected to a mosque, and it is from this that the muezzin calls people. Some mosques have as many as six minarets.

Because Iran is an OPEC (Organization of Petroleum Exporting Countries) country, has lots of oil, is in the Middle East, and is Islamic, many people think that Iranians are Arabs. Although Iran has an Arabic minority and also a substantial Kurdish population, the vast majority of Iranians are Persians, not Arabs. They speak Farsi, which uses the Arabic alphabet but is a different language. (Many languages use the same alphabet that English-speaking people do without speaking English, such as French, German, and Spanish.)

Iran spent almost ten years in a war with its neighbor Iraq. During that time, from 1980 to 1988, thousands of young soldiers on both sides lost their lives. Neither side ultimately won the war.

Iran today is a major producer of oil and natural gas. The city of Abadan is famous for its huge oil refinery. There are oil wells in the fields near Ahvaz. Oil tankers laden with the "black gold" sail through the Persian Gulf and the Strait of Hormuz before shipping the oil off to the world. Iran also is known for its manufacture of plastics, cement, textiles, and clothing. It is most famous for the beautiful and valuable Persian carpets, a traditional art form in Iran for centuries. Kerman, also spelled Kirman, has been the center of highly sophisticated carpet-making since the 1500s.

Other Facts About Iran

- The Strait of Hormuz is a narrow channel that links the Persian Gulf with the Gulf of Oman and the Arabian Sea. It also separates Iran from the Arabian Peninsula. It is of enormous strategic and economic importance because of the oil tankers that pass through it.

- Shah 'Abbas the Great made Isfahan his capital in 1598, and he rebuilt it into one of the largest and most beautiful cities of the seventeenth century. Shah Square, an enormous construction, is at the center of the city.

- Tehran has been the capital city of Iran since 1788. During the nearly forty years that Shah Pahlavi was in power, Tehran underwent drastic modernization.

- The city of Qom was sacred in early Shi'a Islam because Fatimah, the sister of the imam, died there. It was also the home of the Ayatollah Khomeini.

- Qazvin, a region northwest of Tehran, is known for cement production. Qazvin was once the capital of the Safavid Empire.

- Mashhad is the birthplace of Muhammad Taqi Bahar, considered one of the greatest early twentieth-century Iranian poets.

- Rasht is a city known as a cultural center.

- Qanats are underground water supply systems that are still in use in Iran for irrigation. They've been used there for the last 2,500 years.

- If you buy sturgeon in Iran, there's nothing fishy about using rials.

- In Iranian art, main stairways were flanked by glazed pottery animals that were supposed to guard the house and its treasures. These guardians were portrayed as either bulls or griffins.

ISRAEL

There is only one nation in the world that is predominantly Jewish. In the southwest corner of the fertile crescent, Israel occupies one of the most historic areas of the globe. Often called the Near East, the region of the Middle East where Israel is located borders the Mediterranean Sea. Where else can you light a Hanukkah menorah in the holy city of Jerusalem, eat matzohs in Tel Aviv, spin a dreidl in Yafo, or eat a kosher hot dog in Beersheba? Only in Israel.

Israel is on a low coastal plain. The Plain of Sharon is the most densely populated section of the Mediterranean coastal plain. Ramat Gan, Tel Aviv, and Yafo are cities on the Plain of Sharon. The southern half of the country is occupied by the Negev Desert. Because much of Israel is dry land, the Israelis have learned to irrigate very carefully with what little water is available to them. The National Water Carrier system is composed of pipelines and conduits that bring water from northern and central Israel to the Negev.

Agriculture is efficient in Israel. About fourteen percent of the

people work on the land, and half of these live either in kib-
butzim or in moshavim. A kibbutz is a collective farm, and a
moshav is a cooperative farm.

There are many bodies of water in and around Israel. The Dead
Sea lies between Israel and its neighbor Jordan. The Jordan
River forms the boundary between Israel and Jordan. Israel's
southernmost city, the port of Elat, is on the Gulf of Aqaba, in
the Red Sea. The Sea of Galilee, farther north than the Dead
Sea, is near Nazareth, the town where Jesus was raised.

The land where Israel is found today has religious significance
to three of the major religions of the world—Christianity,
Judaism, and Islam. Jerusalem, the major city in Israel, is called
the Holy City because of its history and the many historic and
sacred sites it contains. The Dome of the Rock is a central
shrine in Islam. It is located, along with the Al-Aqsa Mosque, on
the Temple Mount. The Temple Mount is the site of Solomon's
Temple. There is also the Wailing Wall (sometimes called the
Western Wall), which is a sacred site in Judaism, and the inner city
of Old Jerusalem. Until 1948, Yafo Gate (sometimes spelled Jaffa
Gate) was the principal entrance to the Old City. It is located
near the Tower of David.

Israel was created as a nation in 1948. Before that, it was called
Palestine and was occupied by various nations, most notably
the British. Its population was predominantly Arab. Jewish
immigration from Europe began in the late 1800s with the
Zionist movement, and the country was flooded with Jewish
immigrants fleeing the Nazis before the Second World War.
Following a civil war, during which many thousands of
Palestinian Arabs were forced out or fled the country, Israel
declared itself a state and the homeland of the Jewish people.

Although there are Jews living all over the world, they are the majority only in Israel. Modern-day Israelis speak Hebrew. Jewish customs, such as observing holidays like Hanukkah, Yom Kippur, and Passover, can be practiced without fear of persecution. There are many synagogues (temples) in Israel. There are also yeshivas, where Jewish people can study the Talmud, the holy scripture of Judaism. Jewish spiritual leaders are called rabbis.

Since 1948, Israel has engaged in several wars with its Arab neighbors. As a result of 1967's Six Day War, Israel annexed Jordanian and Syrian lands, as well as Egypt's Sinai Peninsula. Israeli Prime Minister Menachem Begin signed a peace treaty with Egypt's Anwar Sadat in 1978 in order to achieve peace between the two nations. The Sinai was returned in 1982. Only in the 1990s have there been talks about permitting the independence of the occupied Palestinian territories, the West Bank and the Gaza Strip. These are crowded, small strips of land separate from each other. They are somewhat like Native American reservations.

Israel today is known for its contributions to the diamond industry, as well as for its chemicals, electronics, and textiles. Netanya is the center for diamond cutting and polishing. Israel also has a fishing industry.

Other Facts About Israel

- Israel is one of the world's largest weapons manufacturers.

- The Mount of Olives, a limestone ridge just east of the Old City of

Jerusalem, is mentioned in both the Old Testament and the New Testament.

- Mount Zion was the easternmost of the two hills of ancient Jerusalem. King David of Israel established it as his royal capital in the tenth century B.C.

- Haifa is the main port city of Israel.

- The ruins of Masada, the mountaintop fortress in southeast Israel, are all that is left of the Jews' last stand against the conquering Romans. Jerusalem fell to the Romans in A.D. 70. Masada occupies the whole top of a huge mesa near the Dead Sea coast.

- The Knesset is the Israeli parliament.

- Israelis spend shekels on tickets to hear the Israel Philharmonic play.

- The Jewish holiday of Passover is a reminder of the exodus of the Jews from Egypt.

ITALY

Its cultural legacy is unparalleled in Western civilization, featuring some of the greatest artists of all time. Its cuisine has spread around the world. It looks like a boot. What is it? It's Italy, the center of the Roman Empire and, later, of the Renaissance, two of the greatest and most colorful periods of history in the West.

If the myths are to be believed, Rome was founded by two brothers, Romulus and Remus, who were raised by wolves. Well . . . maybe so, but there's evidence that Italy was inhabited as far back as the time of the Neanderthals.

Although early accounts are unclear, it is generally believed that the city of Rome, which was built on seven hills, was established in the year 753 B.C. By the year 509 B.C., the republic that became the Roman Empire was established. By A.D. 180, nearly 700 years later, the Roman Empire extended from Britain to North Africa to the Black Sea.

The Romans left a powerful legacy. Their code of laws has formed the basis for the systems we use today. The same is true of their alphabet and their road building, which was so advanced that many of the old Roman roads still exist today. Many of the languages of the world, including Italian, Spanish, French, and Romanian, trace their roots back to the Latin spoken by the Romans, and studying ancient Latin is still considered a part of a true liberal education. The Romans also excelled in areas of plumbing and hygiene, building many sewage systems, dams, and aqueducts. Their architecture was borrowed from the Greeks, as were their gods, but they expanded on the Grecian themes to build great structures like the Coliseum and numerous palaces. What remains today, however, are mostly bridges, roads, and aqueducts left behind by the Romans.

During a period of civil war, Julius Caesar became dictator, with full power over Rome, but he was assassinated in 44 B.C. His adopted son, Octavius, later called Augustus Caesar, eventually became the first emperor (or caesar) of Rome, in 31 B.C., after defeating rival Marc Antony in battle. The caesars of Rome were worshiped as gods, and most of them were beloved by the people. Notable exceptions were Caligula and Nero, two cruel and twisted men who were so hated that the records of their reigns were removed from official Roman histories.

It was in the reign of Tiberius that Jesus was crucified, and it wasn't until the year 313 that Christianity was officially tolerated in an edict issued by Constantine I.

The Roman Empire was eventually overrun by barbarian invaders in the fourth and fifth centuries.

The period between the sack of Rome by Alaric the Visigoth in A.D. 410 and the thirteenth century is referred to as the Middle Ages, a comparatively chaotic time in Europe. During the twelfth century, a revival of culture and economics began to take place, and this ultimately led to the Renaissance, one of the most creative periods in Western history. It was during the Renaissance that we saw the Western invention or use of paper, printing, the mariner's compass, and gunpowder. The New World was discovered during this time by Christopher Columbus, an Italian explorer sailing under the Spanish flag.

It was during the twelfth century that Europeans learned to cultivate beans, which, in turn, made a balanced diet available to all social classes for the first time. Amazing how something as small as a bean can change the course of a civilization. . . .

The Renaissance was personified by the great artist/inventor/musician Leonardo da Vinci. Leonardo's painting the *Mona Lisa* is certainly one of the most famous in the world. He made detailed anatomical drawings and his sketches include ideas for tanks and flying machines. In many ways Leonardo was centuries ahead of his time.

But Leonardo was not alone. The Italian Renaissance represented a virtual explosion of talent. Did you know that all of the Teenage Mutant Ninja Turtles—Raphael, Donatello, Leonardo, and Michaelangelo—were named after great Renaissance painters? Michaelangelo, in particular, is famous for his sculptures and his breathtaking painting on the ceiling of the Sistine Chapel in the Vatican. But there were even more great Italian Renaissance painters, such as Botticelli and Titian. The list goes on and on.

In the early part of the Renaissance, Dante Alighieri wrote *The Divine Comedy*, one of the great works of Western literature. Late in the Renaissance, Galileo turned the world on its ear with new scientific methods and discoveries. He repeated Nicolaus Copernicus's assertion that Earth revolved around the sun (Galileo was later brought up before the Inquisition and forced to deny what he had said), and he published new insights on the concept of gravity. Galileo is often considered to be the founder of modern experimental methods.

In modern times, Italy continues to have a great impact on our world. Foods like pizza, ravioli, spaghetti, fettuccini, and lasagne come from Italy. Italy has also turned out great film-makers like Federico Fellini, whose movie *8½* is a classic, and actors like Marcello Mastroianni and Sophia Loren. Another famous Italian is opera singer Luciano Pavarotti.

Other Facts About Italy

- The Medici family of Florence was one of the most powerful families in Europe during the time of the Renaissance.

- Florence was built to control one of the few north–south crossings of the Arno River. It became a center of Renaissance art and is still one of the best places to go to research or experience that time in history.

- The Leaning Tower of Pisa leans over seventeen feet from the perpendicular because its foundation is settling.

- Rome is famous for its fountains, most notably for the Fountain of the Rivers in the Piazza Navona and the Fontanna di Trevi, which was built in 1762.

- Venice is the Italian coastal city that is famous for its canals and water taxis, and for the beautiful Piazza San Marco. People love to ride the gondolas through the canals, with the gondolier pushing the boat through the water and under the picturesque bridges of the city.

- Naples is located in southern Italy, near the great volcano Mount Vesuvius, which last erupted in 1944. Naples was once a great port city, but it is now in decline. People from Naples are called Neapolitans.

- Bologna has been inhabited since the fourth century B.C. Today the city still carries the flavor of its Roman heritage. The University of Bologna, founded in the eleventh century, is one of the oldest and most famous universities in Europe.

- Verona is located at the foot of the Lessini Mountains, sixty-five miles west of Venice. It is partially encircled by the Adige River. Verona was founded by an ancient tribe. It became a Roman colony in 89 B.C.

- The ancient city of Pompeii was destroyed by Mount Vesuvius in A.D. 79, and modern archaeologists have learned a great deal about ancient Romans from its ruins, which were preserved in the volcanic ash.

- Milan is located in the north of Italy, along the Po River. It was probably first settled around 600 B.C., and has had a long and turbulent history leading into modern times. Today Milan is one of the principal manufacturing and financial centers of Italy.

- Parma is full of churches with important works of art from the Renaissance and earlier. It was also the birthplace of the famous conductor Arturo Toscanini.

- The northern Italian town of Ravenna was once the capital of the Western Roman Empire, but this was late in the history of the Romans (in the fifth century A.D.). It was also the capital of Ostrogothic and Byzantine Italy during the sixth to the eighth centuries.

- Sardinia is the second-largest island in the western Mediterranean. It is located very near the French island of Corsica. The earliest recorded residents of Sardinia were the ancient Phoenicians, though mysterious basalt fortresses called nuraghi predate the Phoenicians.

- Sicily is the largest of the Mediterranean islands, and the most densely populated. Evidence suggests that Sicily was occupied as long as 10,000 years ago. Today, with a few nearby islands, it is an autonomous (self-governing) region of Italy. The highest active volcano in Europe, Mount Etna, is found on Sicily. The Mafia originated in Sicily in the Middle Ages and remains a significant force in island government and culture.

- Although Italy is a Mediterranean country, it is surrounded by smaller seas such as the Ionian, Adriatic, Tyrrhenian, and Ligurian.

- Classical opera first began in Florence. Great Italian composers include Claudio Monteverdi, Alessandro Scarlatti, Gioacchino Rossini, Giuseppe Verdi, and Giacomo Puccini.

- If you're leaving your villa to hear one of Rossini's operas, don't forget to pack a load of lire.

- The popular dance the tarantella was once thought to be a cure for a condition called tarantism, which made people want to dance and was thought to be caused by the bite of the tarantula.

JAPAN

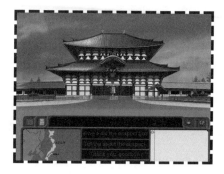

For an island nation smaller than California, Japan sure keeps busy! World famous for its production of electronics and automobiles, Japan also has the largest fishing industry in the world. Maybe that's why it is the home of sushi. The main island, Honshu, contains Japan's largest cities, including the port cities of Kobe and Yokohama, the old capital of Kyoto, and the modern capital, Tokyo. On the island of Hokkaido, to the north, is the city of Sapporo, which was home to the 1972 Winter Olympics.

Japan may be called the Land of the Rising Sun, but it's also the land of earthquakes; there are more than 7,000 tremors a year. That's because Japan's mountains are relatively recent, geologically speaking, and are still growing. At least sixty volcanoes have been active within historic times.

The land is young, but Japanese culture is very old. The original religion of the Japanese people is called Shinto. Shintoism teaches respect for ancestors and nature. Buddhism also flourishes in Japan, especially the homegrown variety called Zen.

Japan is famous for many things, including the huge Sumo wrestlers, sometimes weighing over 400 pounds, who try to knock their opponents off their feet; and the grace of the miniature trees called bonsai. Historically, Japan was famous for the hospitality of women called geishas. The Japanese word geisha literally means "art person," and singing, dancing, and playing the samisen (a lutelike instrument) are indispensable talents for geishas, who are usually exquisitely dressed in traditional silk kimonos.

Early Japanese culture was built around a feudal system and the honor of the samurai, the sword-wielding fighters.

For centuries Japan was known as a military power in Asia. In modern times Japanese forces joined the Germans and the Italians in the Second World War. They waged a brutal island war in the Pacific Ocean and even bombed the U.S. base at Pearl Harbor, Hawaii. Japan surrendered after atomic bombs were dropped on the cities of Hiroshima and Nagasaki.

For more than 1,000 years, from 794 to 1868, Kyoto ("Capital City") was the capital of Japan and the center of Buddhist culture and the arts. Near the end of the Second World War the Americans came close to choosing Kyoto as the target for the first atomic bomb, but one American general had studied in Kyoto before the war and convinced the others to spare it.

Today Japan is a fascinating blend of old and new. Tokyo's ultramodern Ginza entertainment district is not far from the imperial splendor of Edo Castle, once the home of Japan's medieval rulers, called shoguns.

Japanese students are expected to work very hard to pass the difficult examinations after high school that are usually crucial in determining career success.

Other Facts About Japan

- The famous "Bullet Train" travels the Tokaido line between Tokyo and Osaka at 130 miles an hour.

- The popular tempura method of deep-frying food was learned from Portuguese traders who came to Japan in the sixteenth century.

- Japanese money is called yen.

- The Seven Great Temples of Nara, for a time the ancient capital, date from the eighth century. The Todai Temple (745–752) is noted for the Daibutsu, or Great Buddha, a giant statue about fifty feet high that is housed in the Great Buddha hall, one of the largest wooden buildings in the world.

- The Japanese enjoy meandering down the Philosopher's Walk, a 1.3-mile footpath along a canal that leads to the Ginkaku Temple.

- Japanese love a good show, and their staging techniques developed far earlier than did those of the West. By the time of Shakespeare, for instance, the Japanese had already invented a revolving stage, trapdoors, and complex lighting effects. The best-known kinds of Japanese theater are the Noh and the Kabuki.

- The Japanese flag is a red circle on a white background, symbolizing the sun.

- Mount Fuji in the south is the highest mountain in the country at 12,388 feet. Its name means "everlasting life."

- After Japan's defeat in the Second World War, its new constitution was written by the United States.

- Many of the Japanese arts are famous for their refined delicacy, such as the paper-folding art of origami, the art of flower arrangement known as ikebana, and the distinctively short form of poetry called haiku.

KENYA

If someone gave you a pith helmet and you were going on safari, where would you go? Somewhere in Africa, no doubt. A place where you might find elephants, rhinoceroses, zebras, hippopotamuses, gazelles, impalas, antelopes, and other creatures ranging over the vast savanna or clustering around a river or a watering hole. One of your first choices would be Kenya, located between Lake Victoria, Africa's largest lake, and the Indian Ocean.

Kenya is located in the eastern part of Africa, right at the equator. Looking at a map of Africa, you'll see Kenya just south of the great peninsula that juts out to the east, the Horn of Africa.

One of Kenya's main industries is agriculture, with tea and coffee the leading crops, but tourism is a rapidly expanding source of revenue.

Although the official languages of Kenya are Swahili and English, there are more than thirty different ethnic groups in

Kenya, each distinguished by its language and culture. Among those groups are the Kikuyu, the Luhya, the Luo, and the Meru. Of particular note are the Masai, who have become well known to the Western world. The Masai are an ancient nomadic herding tribe with a reputation as fierce warriors. Their diet consists almost entirely of meat, and milk mixed with cow's blood.

Other Facts About Kenya

- Lake Nakaru is located in the Great Rift Valley. It is known as a habitat for many bird species as well as hippopotamuses, waterbucks, and impalas.

- Among the important wildlife parks in Kenya are Marsabit, Masai Mara, and the Tsavo National Park, the largest park in Kenya, located at the foot of Mount Kilimanjaro.

- Mount Elgon is located at the border of Kenya and Uganda. In recent history, Mount Elgon was the location of some of the events of the best-selling book *The Hot Zone*, which dealt with the emergence of the deadly Ebola virus.

- Nairobi, the capital of Kenya, took its name from a waterhole known to the Masai as Enkare Nairobi ("Cold Water").

- Mombasa is located on a small coral island and is linked to the Kenyan mainland by a causeway, bridge, and ferry. It was originally founded in the eleventh century by Arab traders. Although a part of the city and old port are heavily influenced by Arabic culture, there are also several Roman Catholic cathedrals and even a Hindu temple in the city. A newer port serves modern trade and transport needs.

- Located on the shores of Lake Victoria, Kisumu is an important trade center, linked to Mombasa via rail.

- The Tana River is the longest river in Kenya, flowing from Mount Kenya to the Indian Ocean. One of its main attractions is the 440-foot Kitaru ("Seven Forks") Falls.

- The Athi River intersects the Galana River in southern Kenya. The two are often referred to as the Athi-Galana system.

- Jomo Kenyatta was the first president of Kenya. He was prime minister for a year (1963–1964), then was elected president in 1964.

- The famous book *Out of Africa* was written by Danish author Isak Dinesen about her experiences in Kenya. *Out of Africa* was made into a movie starring Meryl Streep.

- When they go out to the movies, Kenyans buy their tickets with shillings.

MEXICO

When he was asked what his newly won empire looked like, Spanish conquistador Hernando Cortés crumpled a piece of parchment and said, "This is a map of Mexico." Two thirds of this country consist of highlands and steep mountains. The rest is either coastal lowlands or the great Sonoran Desert in the north.

Visitors today may come to Mexico for the long sand beaches of Acapulco, or such treats as mariachi bands or the Ballet Folklorico, but they soon become absorbed in the rich historical fabric of this fascinating country. The Mayans, living in temple cities such as Chichén Itzá on the Yucatán Peninsula, had a very sophisticated understanding of mathematics, as the famous Mayan calendar demonstrated. They also came up with the concept of zero.

The Egyptians weren't the only ancients who built pyramids. Still standing in Teotihuacán, whose Nahuatl name means "where men become gods," are the Pyramid of the Sun and the Pyramid of the Moon. In the early 1500s, when a small group of

Spanish adventurers led by Cortés landed near Veracruz, the Aztecs had become the rulers of Mexico. Legend has it they founded their capital city, Tenochtitlán, on a small island in Lake Texcoco, where their elders spotted an eagle, symbol of the sun, holding a snake in its claws. Today this image is found on the Mexican peso.

Cortés, and the Spanish who followed, found Mexico to be a rich land: gold in the Sierra Madre, silver in the mines of Taxco, and copper from Monterrey. More recently, oil has been discovered off the Gulf of Mexico near Tampico.

Mexico City, built over the ruins of the Aztec city of Tenochtitlán, demonstrates the challenges that the country faces today. The capital city is the largest in the world, and one of the most densely populated. The many industries produce dangerous levels of smog. There is also rising discontent with the longtime political dominance of one ruling party, especially among the large Indian population in the south.

Other Facts About Mexico

- Mexico is such a populous country, it has many more Spanish-speaking people than Spain.

- Mexican painting achieved international renown during the twentieth century, when painters such as Diego Rivera became famous for their wall-sized public murals.

- Forty-five miles southeast of Mexico City lies the perpetually snowcapped volcanic peak of Popocatepetl, rising to a height of 17,930 feet.

- On May 5, 1862, a battle was fought at Puebla between the Mexican army and French forces sent by Napoleon III. The

Mexicans won, and the date has become a national holiday of independence, known as Cinco de Mayo ("Fifth of May").

- Tourism is a major growth industry and Mexico's second-largest economic asset after petroleum, with world-famous resorts such as Acapulco, Ixtapa-Zihuatanejo, Cancún, Cozumel, Mazatlán, and Cabo San Lucas.

- Oaxaca was the home of Benito Juárez and Porfirio Díaz, two of Mexico's most famous presidents, and is noted for its sixteenth-century art and architecture.

- The Colegio San Nicolás, founded in 1540 in Pátzcuaro and moved to Morelia in 1580, is the oldest institution of higher learning in Mexico.

- Jalapa was a thriving Indian village when Hernando Cortés marched through it in 1519. It became famous in colonial days for its annual fair, filled with the goods brought from Cádiz, in Spain, by the returning Spanish silver fleet.

- Aguascalientes is sometimes called La Ciudad Perforada ("The Perforated City") because of a labyrinth of tunnels underneath it. They were excavated beneath the city in pre-Columbian times by an unknown tribe.

MOROCCO

If you're traveling in Europe and want a taste of something exotic, try taking the ferry from Spain past the Rock of Gibraltar to the Arabic culture of Morocco. Your first taste of this different world is Tangier, a favorite locale of American beatniks in the 1950s. Try the mint tea—it's the national drink.

If you have an interest in history, travel to Fez, a center of Islamic learning since the eleventh century. For many centuries Fez was the only source of the distinctive brimless hat called, not coincidentally, the fez. If it's movie history you seek, go to Morocco's largest port, Casablanca, and try to find Rick's Café Americain, where Humphrey Bogart said, "Here's looking at you, kid," to Ingrid Bergman, and where Sam played it again. Casablanca is also the site of the largest mosque in Africa, the Hassan II Mosque.

If you like shopping, head straight for the souk, or bazaar, in Marrakech, which has one of the most colorful marketplaces in Morocco. And if you're one of those people who like to see where politicians work their magic, head for Rabat, the nation's capital. After that, you'll probably be ready for some open spaces, so how about the Atlas Mountains, with the highest African peak above the equator, Jebel Toubkal, at 13,665 feet?

Morocco was originally settled by a nomadic people called Berbers. They were conquered by the Arabs in the 600s and an Arab-Berber empire was formed. In the eleventh and twelfth centuries, most of Spain and all of northwest Africa was ruled by the Berbers, from Morocco. The Berbers gave their name to the Barbary Coast. For many centuries pirates from these shores demanded tribute (payment) from European ships in exchange for not attacking them.

Moorish influence spread all through Europe. Its influences can be seen in architectural styles, or heard in the music of Spain and southern France. A prince of Morocco was even included as a character in Shakespeare's play *The Merchant of Venice*. In modern times, Morocco has been a protectorate of France. The French called the country "Le Maroc," or land of the Moors. Morocco didn't become independent from France until 1956.

Morocco is largely a desert land, with the hot winds, called siroccos, that roar off the Sahara toward the sea. The main crop is olives, and Morocco is the world's largest exporter of phosphate rock, used in fertilizers.

Other Facts About Morocco

- One of the centers of Morocco's large olive industry is the ancient city of Meknes, whose palaces and mosques earned for this one-time capital city the name "Versailles of Morocco."

- When in Morocco, if you accept an invitation to be taken to the Kasbah, you'll find yourself in the old, fortified section of the city.

- The ancient port city of Safi was originally settled by the Canaanites.

- If Horace Greeley had been an Arab, he might have said, "Go maghreb, young man, go maghreb!" Maghreb is Arabic for "west," and no Arab country is farther west than Morocco.

- In 1960 the city of Agadir was virtually destroyed by two earthquakes, a tidal wave, and a fire, which killed about 12,000 people.

- The Rif Mountains hug the Mediterranean Sea almost the full length of Morocco, leaving only a few narrow coastal valleys suitable for agriculture or cities.

- Though geographically connected to Morocco at the Mediterranean entrance to the Strait of Gibraltar, the eight-square-mile territory of Ceuta is administered by Spain.

- Morocco's currency, the dirham, has a picture of Morocco's King Hassan on it.

- The capital city of Rabat was founded in the twelfth century by 'Abd al-Mu'min, the first Almohad ruler, as a ribat ("camp") at which to quarter the troops for his jihad ("holy war") against Spain. The third Almohad sultan, Abu Yusuf Ya'qub al-Mansur, built the famous tower of Hassan, which is still standing.

- Don't forget the popcorn when you see *Blue Men of the Sahara: Tribal Life on the Sahara,* a film presenting a study on nomadic Arab tribal life in southern Morocco.

- Muhammed V, sultan of Morocco from 1927 to 1957, secured Moroccan independence from French colonial rule, and then ruled as king from 1957 to 1961.

- The annual commercial and religious fair in Tan-Tan attracts traders and nomads from as far away as Senegal and Marrakech; camels and sheep are exchanged for grains, tea, sugar, and other necessities.

NEPAL

This country is bound to pique your interest, but you'll be walking in thin air as you explore its highest points. Seven of its mountains reach above 26,000 feet, and Mount Everest, the highest of the high, tops out at 29,028 feet! Maybe that's why they call this country the Rooftop of the World.

This is Nepal, the world's only officially Hindu country. Although Nepal is officially Hindu, many Buddhists live there, and travelers will encounter many stupas, special pagodas dedicated to the Buddha and to Buddhist rituals. Of course, the really observant may get a glimpse of the legendary yeti, otherwise known as the abominable snowman.

Nepal is mostly surrounded by Chinese Tibet to the north and India to the south. It has no access to oceans or seas, though a few rivers run through it, such as the Kosi, the Narayani, and the Karnali.

Nepal is a favorite location for mountain climbers, who challenge themselves in the dangerous environments of Everest and Annapurna. With the help of the native Sherpa, who are used to living at these amazingly high elevations, the climbers attempt to weather the weather, so to speak, and make it to the top. Climbing Himalayan peaks is very dangerous, however, and just preparing for one of these climbs can take months.

Some people like to enjoy the natural beauty of the Himalayas, but don't want to risk their lives by climbing to the tops of the mountains. These people, who are called trekkers, will hike through the plateaus and valleys of the Himalayas, sometimes for weeks at a time, but won't attempt the dangerous climbs to the top.

The Sherpa are simple people who live without industry or modern conveniences. They herd yaks, which are great cowlike creatures that provide meat, milk, and hides. Even the dung of the yak is used as fuel, because in the high elevations there isn't anything else to burn. Yaks are also used to carry heavy loads in the relatively lower elevations, though even yaks can't make it to the tops of the mountains. Wild yaks are considered an endangered species now, and are found only in Tibet.

Other Facts About Nepal

- Not all of Nepal is mountainous. The Tarai is a fertile, marshy plain that runs parallel to the Himalayan range and extends into India. Several rivers run through it. The Tarai plain ranges from 600 to 1,200 feet above sea level, in contrast with the mountain range nearby.

- Kathmandu is the capital of Nepal. It was first established in the year 723. Its original name was Manju-Patan, which means "wooden temple." Kathmandu is at an elevation of 4,344 feet—the foothills of the Himalayas—near the confluence of two rivers, the Baghmati and the Vishnumati.

- Annapurna is actually a massive mountain with four peaks. Two of the peaks, Annapurna I and Annapurna II, reach above 26,000 feet. Although climbers had previously reached 28,150 feet on Everest, in 1950 Annapurna I was the first mountain higher than 26,000 feet to be climbed all the way to its summit. In 1970, an all-woman team of Japanese climbers reached the summit of Annapurna III.

- In the city of Bhaktapur in central Nepal is an old palace in Durbar Square. The palace is known for its fine wood carvings.

- The town of Pashupati is considered one of the holiest places in Nepal, and its ancient temple, the shrine of Pashupatinath, is devoted to the worship of the Hindu god Shiva. The annual Shivaratri festival attracts seekers from India and other countries.

- Tourism is a growing industry in Nepal. Among the areas that benefit from tourism are Pokhara, the area around Mount Everest, and the Narayani area, where there is big game.

- The Siwalik Hills are sometimes called the Siwalik Range or the Outer Himalayas. Though only around 3,000 to 4,000 feet in height, this range extends for 1,000 miles, through India, Nepal, and Pakistan. The name Siwalik means "belonging to Shiva."

- From the tenth through the eighteenth centuries, the Malla dynasty ruled in what is now Nepal. In the 1400s, they divided their territories into three independent principalities: Kathmandu, Patan, and Bhaktpur. They were conquered in 1769 by the Gurkha, who established their capital in Kathmandu.

- The town of Gurkha was the original home of the Gurka people, the ancestors of the modern fighting forces still known as the Gurkhas.

- The Gurkhas are notorious for their fighting abilities and many of them are enlisted in the British and Indian armies. Often, when the Gurkas return home to Nepal after serving in the military, they become teachers and community leaders.

- The curved knife of the Gurkas is called a kukri knife. It is named after the hind teeth of a particular variety of snake called the kukri.

- Mount Kanchenjunga, the world's third-highest mountain, gets its name from a Tibetan phrase that translates as "five treasures of the great snow."

- Despite overcutting and poor management, timber is one of the most important resources and sources of revenue in Nepal. About one third of the country is forested.

- Mount Manaslu, sometimes called Kutang I, stands 26,781 feet high at the summit and was first scaled in 1956.

- Nepalese rupees will get you some tea or dahl, a thick lentil soup or stew, in a restaurant in Kathmandu.

- When you're in Nepal, you'll find lots of shamans—spiritual teachers and guides—to point you toward nirvana, the blissful state of enlightenment and freedom from rebirth.

- The Temple of Swayambunath is a Buddhist shrine on the western outskirts of Kathmandu.

- The rolling hills near Ramechhap are called Mahabharat Lekh.

- Remains of a human species called ramapithecus have been found in Patan, a city south of Kathmandu. There is also a town in India called Patan.

THE NETHERLANDS

Remember the story of the little boy who put his finger in the dike? That could happen only in the Netherlands, where half the country would be underwater without the dikes that keep the ocean out of land below sea level. That's why the Netherlands is called one of the Low Countries. It's also often called Holland, although this name really applies only to two provinces along the North Sea. And as if that wasn't confusing enough, the people of the Netherlands are called Dutch!

Two things that the Netherlands are known for are windmills and tulips. When the Dutch people reclaimed the land from the sea, they used windmills to pump the seawater beyond the dikes. Then, after treating the land to remove the salt, they planted tulips. The reclaimed land is called the Polders, which are protected by a long range of coastal sand dunes.

But flowers are not what once allowed the Dutch East India Company, in the seventeenth century, to control its huge empire. It stretched from New York City (then called New Amsterdam, after the Dutch capital) to the Caribbean island of Aruba, and all the way to Indonesia. Due to its daring sea explorers and shrewd merchants, the Netherlands established extensive colonial holdings and became the leading commercial nation in Europe. The oldest stock exchange in the world is in Amsterdam.

But the Dutch people are not all merchants. The famous philosopher Benedict de Spinoza made glass lenses in Amsterdam while developing his Rationalist theories. Speaking of lenses, the microscope was invented by Antonie van Leeuwenhoek, who sold cloth for a living but became the first person to peer into the tiny world of what he called "animalcules." Some of the most famous paintings in the world are by the Dutchmen Rembrandt van Rijn and Vincent van Gogh, and can be seen in Amsterdam's Rijksmuseum. Other prominent natives of the Netherlands include the Arctic explorer Willem Barents and Abel Tasman, who discovered Tasmania.

The Netherlands was invaded by Germany in the Second World War, and the port city of Rotterdam was nearly destroyed by bombing. Anne Frank and her Jewish family hid from the Nazis in Amsterdam, and her diary provides a chilling reminder of the terror of those times.

Other Facts About the Netherlands

- The money of the Netherlands is called guilders.

- The Netherlands is not the best place to sell automobiles: Besides all the boats on the canals, there are three times more bicycles than cars.

- The annual (March to May) flower exhibition, held on a former country estate around the seventeenth-century De Keukenhof Castle, consists of gardens covering sixty-five acres.

- Its original Roman name, Trajectum ad Rhenum (Ford on the Rhine), later became Ultrajectum, and then Utrecht, where the Netherlands' largest state university was founded in 1636.

- The town of Edam is famous for its red-coated Edam cheese, as the town of Gouda is famous for its semi-soft cheese traditionally made in flat wheels weighing ten to twelve pounds.

- The province of Flevoland consists of three polders, or areas reclaimed from the sea, and is typical of the Dutch provinces crisscrossed by canals.

- The seat of government is the Hague, which is also where the International Court of Justice hears legal cases of global importance.

- One of the world's largest companies is Philips, located in Eindhoven, which got its start making lightbulbs.

- The town of Delft is famous for its tin-glazed earthenware, as well as for being the birthplace of the painter Jan Vermeer.

- The Dutch name for Santa Claus is Sinterklass. The tradition of giving gifts in honor of St. Nicholas came to the New World when the Dutch established the colony of New Amsterdam, later named New York City.

- The Treaty on European Union, bringing greater unity to many European countries, was concluded in Maastricht in December 1991.

- Since 1980, Queen Beatrix has occupied the royal throne, and has given birth to the first male heirs of the House of Orange since 1890.

- The ice-skating race called the Elfstedentocht, or "Eleven Towns' Race," takes place in the far-north province of Friesland, where the Frisians have maintained both their own language and their own literature to a considerable degree.

NEW ZEALAND

N ew Zealand has been called the most out-of-the-way nation on earth. It has two main islands: North and South, separated by the twenty-mile-wide Cook Strait.

New Zealand is a land of fascinating contrasts. The Southern Alps, a 300-mile-long chain of mountains on South Island, contain New Zealand's highest mountain, Mount Cook (12,349 feet), and twenty-two other peaks above 10,000 feet, as well as more than 360 glaciers. Steep rivers such as the Rangitikei tumble down through the Canterbury Plains, some of the richest pasture lands in the world and home to New Zealand's 60 million sheep. (No wonder New Zealand is a world leader in wool exports!) From the Milford Sound to the Doubtful Sound, there are so many fjords you might think you're in Norway.

On North Island, you can go from the top of the dormant volcano, Mount Egmont (8,260 feet), down to the Polynesian beach sands of Ninety Mile Beach. Or you can visit the hot springs, boiling mud pools, and spouting geysers of Rotorua.

People from New Zealand are sometimes called Kiwis, an affectionate reference to the flightless bird, about the size of a chicken, unique to New Zealand. Or maybe it's a reference to the kiwifruit, which also grows in New Zealand.

The original people of New Zealand were the Polynesian Maori. From 1769 to 1770 Captain James Cook circumnavigated and charted the two main islands. Cook's initial contact with the Maori was violent, but later voyages and contacts proved more harmonious. In the early 1880s the development of refrigerated ships made it possible for New Zealand farmers to ship butter, cheese, and meat to Great Britain, helping the islands to prosper.

New Zealand has taken a strong stand against the proliferation of nuclear weapons. Its decision to ban nuclear-powered and nuclear-armed vessels from New Zealand's ports strained relations with the United States, but the people of New Zealand are used to choosing their own course. It was the first country to grant women the right to vote, in 1893.

Other Facts About New Zealand

- The Tasman Glacier is the largest in New Zealand, with a length of eighteen miles and a width of more than one-half mile, flowing down the eastern slopes of Mount Cook.

- The Bay of Plenty was named in 1769 by Captain James Cook, in recognition of the generous provisions and water received from Maoris living along its shore.

- Abel Janszoon Tasman, a Dutch sailor, commanded an expedition that sighted the coast of New Zealand in December 1642. His attempt to land on South Island provoked a clash with the Maori.

- New Zealand's comprehensive welfare system provides benefits for sickness, maternity, old age, disability, widowhood, orphanhood, unemployment, and emergencies. Hospitalization in public institutions is free.

- The name of Lake Wakatipu, a resort area near Queenstown on South Island, may refer to a legend of a goblin living below the surface whose breathing was believed to cause the unusual five-inch rise and fall in the lake's water level.

- One of New Zealand's most famous writers is the short-story writer Katherine Mansfield, born in the capital city of Wellington.

- Lake Wanaka occupies seventy-four square miles of a valley that is dammed by a moraine (glacial debris) and that lies at the eastern foot of the Southern Alps.

- The city of Napier on Hawke Bay is New Zealand's largest wool wholesale center and is also a major resort area.

- The idea that an atom consists of a single positively charged nucleus surrounded by electrons was first put forth by Ernest (later Lord) Rutherford, born near Nelson on the northern tip of South Island.

- The port city of Dunedin was founded in 1848 as a Scottish Free Church settlement. Its name comes from the Gaelic word for Edinburgh (Duneideann). The discovery of gold in 1861 made it New Zealand's leading city during the second half of the nineteenth century.

- Lake Taupo is the largest lake in New Zealand and covers the remains of several craters on the volcanic plateau of central North Island.

- Auckland is the country's largest city and its largest port. It occupies a narrow isthmus of North Island between Waitemata Harbour and Manukau Harbour.

- Some of the earliest battles between Europeans and Maoris centered on the establishment of whaling stations in the 1830s around the present-day location of the city of Marlborough, near Nelson on the northeastern tip of South Island.

NIGERIA

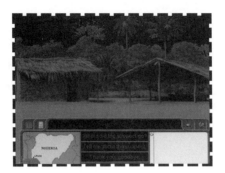

When you think of Nigeria, think of people. One seventh of all African people live in Nigeria, making it the most populous African nation. Over 250 languages are spoken. Nigeria's borders were drawn by colonial powers with no regard for tribal boundaries, resulting in many challenges to national unity.

The Hausa and the Fulani, who farm the northern savannas on the edge of the Sahara, are Muslims, and have little in common with the Ibo and Yoruba tribes of the south. In 1967 civil war broke out when the Ibos declared their region the independent Republic of Biafra, only to surrender three years later after a bitter struggle.

The first Europeans to reach the Nigerian coast were the Portuguese in the fifteenth century. By the seventeenth century British slave ships regularly visited the coast of Nigeria, trading with tribal chiefs along the Niger River delta. Many African-Americans can trace their roots to the Yoruba and Ibo peoples of Nigeria.

Nigeria became a British colony in 1886, gaining its independence in 1960. In 1991, the capital city was moved 300 miles north, from the old slaving center of Lagos to the planned city of Abuja.

Nigeria's estimated petroleum and natural gas reserves represent nearly one third of Africa's total reserves, and hold out a promise of wealth to the people of Nigeria, if they can overcome their history of internal conflict and corrupt military governments.

Other Facts About Nigeria

- Hausa is by far the most widely spoken language in Nigeria, and the continued political domination of the country by the Hausa-Fulani group has contributed to its spread. English is the official language of Nigeria but is used mostly in the cities.

- The earliest identified culture in Nigeria is that of the Nok people, who flourished between about 500 B.C. and about A.D. 200 in the area north of the confluence of the Niger and Benue rivers on the Jos Plateau.

- Ibadan, Nigeria's second-largest city after Lagos, is an important commercial center. Virtually every street and corner in the city center is a market square or stall. Similar to the tie-dye cloth found in America, adire cloth is dyed locally in large pots of indigo.

- The northern city of Kano was a main caravan stop for African traders from the Atlantic Ocean to the Nile River. Cowrie shells were used as money. In return for Hausa leatherwork, cloth, and metalwares, Kano received kola nuts from Ghana; salt from the Sahara; slaves from other tribes; natron (a useful mineral) from Lake Chad; and sword blades, weaponry, silk, spices, perfumes, and books brought from Europe by the trans-Saharan camel caravans.

- The Niger River (Africa's third largest) and the Benue, the Niger's largest tributary, are the principal rivers of Nigeria.

- Animal life includes chimpanzees, gorillas, African wild dogs, leopards, elephants, giraffes, lions, crocodiles, and snakes of many species.

- Benin City has long been famous for its bronze sculptures, dating from the thirteenth century, and for its ivory and wood carvings. Today, Benin City is the center of Nigeria's rubber industry.

- Lake Chad, on Nigeria's northeastern border, is the largest lake in western Africa and the remnant of a much larger ancient sea. Crocodiles and hippopotamuses flourish in the lake.

- After the end of the slave trade, the southeastern port of Calabar became an important center for the export of palm oil, ivory, and beeswax, until it was eclipsed by Port Harcourt on the Niger River delta.

- The coastline of Nigeria's Gulf of Guinea corresponds remarkably to the continental edge of Brazil in South America. The similarity was one of the first clues that led scientists to conclude that the two continents were at one time connected.

- The Nigerian currency is called naira.

- The name of the northern city of Kaduna is Hausa for "crocodile."

- Ogbomosho, Nigeria's third-largest city, is inhabited mainly by Yoruba farmers, traders, and artisans. Yams, cassava, corn, and sorghum are grown for export to the cocoa-producing areas of Yorubaland to the south.

- Ife is the most ancient town of the Yoruba people, and is considered by the Yoruba to be a holy city and the mythical birthplace of mankind.

- Camel caravans from the Sahara traveled south to Zaria to exchange salt for slaves, cloth, leather, and grain.

- Sapele has been a center for sawmilling (obeche, abura, sapele, and mahogany) since 1925. Its plywood- and veneer-manufacturing plant is one of the largest in western Africa.

- Formerly a slave-trading center, Warri now refines petroleum and is one of the leading steel producers in Nigeria.

- The cultivation and export of cocoa is the town of Iwo's economic mainstay. Cotton weaving and dyeing (with locally grown indigo) are also traditionally important activities.

- The town of Minna became more of a flourishing community after the opening of the Kano-to-Baro railway (1911) and the extension of the Lagos-to-Jebba line (1915) to a junction in Minna. Minna became a major collecting point for peanuts, cotton, yams, and pigs.

- The northern city of Katsina entered its greatest period of prosperity in the early eighteenth century. Besides being the leading Hausa commercial state, it replaced Timbuktu, in Mali, as the chief West African center of Islamic studies.

- The market village of Maiduguri is located on the north bank of the seasonal Ngadda River, the waters of which disappear in the firki ("black cotton") swamps just southwest of Lake Chad.

PAKISTAN

akistan is a land of diversity. It can be divided into four distinct areas: the Baluchistan Plateau, the Indus Plain, the great highlands, and the desert areas. The people of Pakistan are also diverse, with ethnic heritages derived from various settlers and invaders of the region, including Aryans, Persians, Greeks, Pashtuns, and Moguls. There isn't even a language that can be said to be common to all the people of Pakistan, though the main languages are Punjabi, Sindhi, Pashto, and Baluchi. The official language is Urdu, which is like Hindi but written with the Persian script.

Pakistan's history is complex, especially considering that the country we call Pakistan didn't officially exist as such until the twentieth century. However, human occupation of what is now Pakistan is thought to have begun around 3500 B.C. in the Boluchistan region. After that, a great civilization flourished in the Indus Valley from about 2500 B.C. to about 1500 B.C., when the civilization abruptly ended.

Pakistan was governed at various times by rulers from India or

Persia, and the Indus Valley was even conquered in 327 B.C. by Alexander the Great. Pakistan was variously part of the great Mauryan Empire, and later came under Gupta rule from India. In the eighth century, Muslim conquerors entered Baluchistan.

Pakistan was under Muslim rule of one kind or another from the eighth century until the mid-1700s. That's when the British East India Company took control of the area and ruled until 1858, when the British government took over. Pakistan, which remained primarily Muslim, separated from the rest of India, which was primarily Hindu, in 1947. Pakistan was further divided into East Pakistan and West Pakistan. Disputes over the Kashmir territory resulted in a full-scale war with India in 1965. Then, because most of East Pakistan was Bengali, another split occurred, and East Pakistan became Bangladesh in 1972. At that time, West Pakistan became simply Pakistan.

The capital of Pakistan, Islamabad, or "City of Islam," was named to reflect the Muslim beliefs of the Pakistanis. It was actually designed and constructed beginning in 1961, with help from an international team of architects. Among the buildings in the capital are the Secretariat, Pakistan House, President's House, National Assembly Building, and Grand National Mosque. Two universities were also built, the University of Islamabad and the People's Open University, which was later renamed Allama Iqbal Open University.

Other Facts About Pakistan

- The flag of Pakistan is green with a white star and a crescent moon.

- Pakistan's Indus River runs through the fertile Indus Valley and empties into the Arabian Sea at the Gulf of Kutch.

- In contrast with the fertile Indus region, the Thar Desert, which extends from Pakistan into India, is an arid and barren region where the best mode of transportation is probably a camel. Actually, camels are used for transportation, as pack animals, and even for plowing the land for agriculture. The Thar Desert is also known as the Great Indian Desert.

- A land of contrasts, Pakistan is the location of the second-highest mountain in the world. Located in the Karakoram range, it is called K2 and is 28,250 feet high. Locally, it is called Dapsang or Chogori, and is also sometimes called Mount Godwin Austen, named after the mountain's first surveyor.

- Although there is a state called Punjab in India, Pakistan also has a Punjab. The name means "five waters" and it gets this name from the five rivers that flow through it—the Jhelum, Chenab, Ravi, Beas, and Sutlej, all tributaries of the Indus. Late in the eighteenth century, the religious order called Sikhs gained power in the Punjab, where Sikhism began.

- The Punjab is the most populous area of Pakistan, and features extensive agriculture and industry. Major cities include Lahore, Faisalabad, and Rawalpindi. Most of the population speaks Punjabi, but uses Urdu as the main written language. Among the chief crops grown in the Punjab region are wheat and cotton.

- The Sindh is a region of Pakistan that includes the Indus River delta. Sindh gets its name from the Indus River, in fact, and it is here that a great civilization flourished thousands of years before the birth of Christ. Its capital is Karachi.

- The great mountain range called the Hindu Kush runs along the borders of Pakistan with Afghanistan and China. Passes through this mountain range have had great military significance throughout history as routes to and from the northern plains of India. The most important of those passes is the Khyber Pass, which was used by many of the invaders of the region throughout history.

- The magnificent Shalimar Gardens are located in Lahore, the second-largest city in Pakistan. Built in 1641 by Shah Jahan, these gardens extend over eighty acres of terraced land dotted with fountains.

- The people of Chitral are known to be exceptional horsemen and excel at the game of polo. Chitral was once a center of slave trading because the women of the region were thought to be especially beautiful and were sold to people in Afghanistan and in Peshawar. This practice was stopped when the British came to power.

- The ancient city of Peshawar was once the capital of a Buddhist kingdom and was called Gandhara then. It is located near the Khyber Pass, west of the Bara River. One of its famous bazaars is the Qissah Khwani Bazaar, or "Street of the Storytellers," where foreign merchants would gather to trade their goods. Peshawar got its modern name, which means "frontier town," in the 1500s.

- Near Peshawar is the city of Mardan, and just outside Mardan is the Rock of Shahbazgarhi, which contains a great inscription from the Emperor Ashoka, who lived in the third century B.C.

- Although there is a city called Hyderabad in southern India, there is also a city in Pakistan of the same name. The name was derived from Muhammad's son-in-law, whose name was 'Ali or Haydar. Hyderabad is the third-largest city in Pakistan.

- The origins of the Pashtun tribes are unclear, but they date back many centuries. They claim their ancestry is linked to King Saul of Israel by his grandson, Afghana, but this is not verifiable. At one time, the Pashtun were known as Afghans before the term became applied to anyone who lives in Afghanistan. Although most of the population of Afghanistan is Pashtun, there are actually more Pashtuns in Pakistan, mostly in the Quetta region.

- Quetta is both a city and a district. The city is located up near the Afghani border. It got its name from the Pashto word for fort, kwatkot. It is still known locally as Shal or Shalkot.

- If you're going out to eat dahl and rice or purchase bangles at the local bazaar, bring along some rupees.

- In parts of Pakistan, water buffalo, rather than cows, provide milk.

- In India and Pakistan, most people cook with a clarified butter called ghee. Unlike butter, ghee can be heated to high temperature and doesn't go bad so quickly. Ghee can be made from cow's milk or milk from the water buffalo. Ghee can also be burned in oil lamps.

PANAMA

Panama is famous for its water, specifically, the waterway called the Panama Canal, which connects the Atlantic and Pacific Oceans across the narrow isthmus where North and South America meet. Forty ships a day pass through the Canal via a series of locks that raise and lower the ships like elevators.

The Canal was built by the United States in 1914, and there are many American influences in Panama. The most popular spectator sports in Panama, for instance, are baseball, boxing, horse racing, and basketball, rather than soccer. American currency is often used in addition to the native money, called balboas. Even the Panamanian flag is red, white, and blue, with stars.

When Christopher Columbus landed in Panama in 1502, the land was occupied by the Cuna, Guaymí, Chocó, and other Indian peoples, who hunted with bows and arrows, blowguns, and poisoned darts. Giant anteaters, bush dogs, ocelots, jaguars, tapirs, and American crocodiles are some of the wildlife of Panama.

Vasco de Balboa founded the first Spanish colony in 1510, and a few years later Panama City became the capital. Because it's only about fifty miles from the Atlantic to the Pacific Oceans, many people shipped their goods through Panama rather than sail all the way around the tip of South America. Also, the California gold rush of 1849 brought prosperity, because many prospectors chose the Panamanian route to California instead of the arduous overland U.S. trail.

Panama gained its independence from Spain in 1821, and then became a part of Colombia. The U.S.-financed Panama Railway was opened in 1855 and led directly to the founding of the city of Colón (Spanish for Columbus). A French company originally tried to build a canal across the isthmus in 1879, but its work came to a halt in 1889. Between 1850 and 1900 alone Panama had forty administrations, fifty riots, five attempted secessions from Colombia, and thirteen U.S. interventions. The United States helped Panama secede from Colombia in 1903, in exchange for permission to build the Canal.

Since the late 1960s Panama has developed into a major international financial center, capitalizing on favorable banking laws and the absence of exchange controls. In response to continuing Panamanian requests for more autonomy, the United States signed the Panama Canal Treaty of 1977, agreeing to turn over all Canal operations to Panama in 1999.

Other Facts About Panama

- U.S. forces invaded Panama in 1989 to overthrow the country's ruler, General Manuel Noriega, for criminal activities.

- Panama's highest peak is an inactive volcano, Volcan Barú, at 11,401 feet.

- The city of David, near the Gulf of Chiriqui and Puerto Armuelles on the border with Costa Rica, might be a good place to order some mocha ice cream; its main exports are sugar, coffee, and cocoa.

- The Caribbean coast of Panama is much wetter than the Pacific side, so bring your bug repellant if you plan to visit the Mosquito Gulf.

- The two principal mountain ranges of Panama, the Tabasará Mountains in the west and the Cordillera de San Blas in the east, are separated near the center of the country by the strip of lower land that contains the Canal.

- Ships must be raised and lowered on their journey between oceans by means of locks, such as the three locks on Lake Gatun, eighty-five feet above the Atlantic Ocean.

- The birthrate in Panama is the lowest in Central America.

- Panama is one of the world's largest exporters of bananas.

PERU

When you hear the name Peru, you think of the Incas, who built a powerful empire high in the Andes Mountains. And when you think of the Andes, you think of—the potato? Yes, the potato was unknown to the rest of the world until the Spanish conquistadors brought it back to Europe from Peru (along with plenty of Incan gold)! Even today, in the village marketplaces surrounding the capital city of Lima, you can find over sixty different varieties of potato.

Peru's name comes from a Quechua Indian word meaning "land of abundance." It is the third-largest nation in South America, after Brazil and Argentina. Most of the important cities of Peru, such as Lima, the port city of Callao, Arequipa, and Chiclayo, lie in the coastal lowlands, in the shadows of the Andean cordillera (mountain range). On eastern slopes of the Andes lie humid tropical rain forests, which contain the main headwaters of the Amazon River. Lake Titicaca, in the southern region known as the Altiplano, is the world's highest navigable body of water at 12,500 feet.

There are many high mountains in the Andes, such as the picturesque volcano called El Misti (19,098 feet), but the highest is Mount Huascarán (22,205 feet). It's a dangerous mountain: In 1962 an avalanche there destroyed several villages and killed about 3,500 persons, and in 1970 a severe earthquake caused landslides that buried ten villages; tens of thousands of people were killed in one of the worst natural disasters of the twentieth century.

The railroads in Peru are the highest in the world. The railroad between Lima and Huancayo in the Andes reaches an altitude of 15,885 feet as it crosses one of several mountain passes!

Peruvian civilizations date back about 10,000 years. The Incas established their capital at Cuzco sometime in the twelfth century. Their technology and architecture were highly developed. Their irrigation systems, palaces, temples, and vast network of roads can still be seen throughout the Andes. The Incas ruled for only a few hundred years before Spanish conquistadors, led by Francisco Pizarro, conquered them, helped to a large extent by the very roads the Incas had built. A remnant of the Inca people remained, hidden high in the mountains. The Spanish never found their hideaway, called Machu Picchu, and it was not discovered until 1911, by explorer Hiram Bingham.

Lima is the capital city of Peru. Francisco Pizarro, who conquered the Incas for Spain, founded Lima in 1535. Pizarro was killed by the forces of his own brother. He is reputed to have drawn a cross of his own blood on the ground, kissed it, cried "Jesus," and then fallen dead. His bones are buried in the Lima cathedral, in the main square of the city. The University of San Marcos in Lima, founded in 1551, is the oldest university in South America.

Peru gained its independence along with other South America countries after 300 years of Spanish rule, and until recent times was ruled largely by a succession of military governments. The popularly elected civilian governments in the 1980s and 1990s, however, have been unstable because of skyrocketing inflation and unemployment, a gigantic foreign debt, and violence by guerrilla groups. The guerillas, such as the neo-Maoist Sendero Luminoso ("Shining Path") and the Tupac Amaru Revolutionary Movement, used terrorist tactics. Drug trafficking and wide-spread coca farming also hampered economic reform. These threats led President Alberto K. Fujimori (elected in 1990) to extreme measures in 1992, suspending the constitution and abridging political rights and freedoms.

Before 1972, Peru had been the world's leading fishing nation, with anchovies the main catch. But overfishing, combined with a severe occurrence of El Niño (an irregular variation in weather patterns) that year, depleted the fishing grounds, and the catch plummeted. Through conservation measures, the fishing industry is gradually recovering.

Other Facts About Peru

- Callao, near Lima, is the main port of Peru, and was founded in 1537 by Francisco Pizarro. Simón Bolívar landed there in 1824 to fight for independence against Spain, and three years later it was the scene of Spain's final surrender.

- The Quechua Indians native to the Andes have developed extra-large lungs as an adaptation to the absence of oxygen in the high-altitude air.

- The native weavers of Peru are famous for their brightly colored shawls and caps, whose patterns often indicate the owner's home village and social status.

- Before the Incas, a people called the Nazca lived in southern Peru. Besides their pottery, all that remains are mysterious animal figures and geometric forms scratched into the surface of several desert mesas. The figures, which include straight lines, triangles, spirals, a bird, a monkey, a spider, and flowers, are hundreds of feet in length and can be recognized only from the sky, leading some people to speculate that they were meant to be seen by UFOs.

- Peru is home to such grazing animals as the llama, the alpaca, and the vicuna. The natives weave bright clothing out of their fine-quality wool.

- If you take a dip in the Urubamba River, watch out for the deadly, carnivorous piranha fish. They travel in schools, and with their large jaws and razor-sharp teeth, they can reduce even a large animal to a skeleton in a few minutes.

- The most densely vegetated region of Peru is east of the Andes, with wild rubber, mahogany, cinchona, cocoa, vanilla, and curare trees. In the same Amazon basin are parrots, monkeys, sloths, jaguars, capybaras (the world's largest rodent), and alligators.

- The Andes don't allow much rain to fall in the western portions of Peru, such as in the Sechura Desert.

- Peruvians used to call their money intis, after the Inca sun god, but in 1991 they changed its name to nuevo sol, which translates as "new sun."

THE PHILIPPINES

The Philippines is not just another ordinary island nation on the Southeast Asian side of the Pacific Rim. It's made up of more than 7,000 islands, it's been called the coconut capital of the world, and it's the only predominantly Roman Catholic country in Asia.

The two principal islands of the Philippines are Luzon in the north and Mindanao in the south. Together these two make up two thirds of the land area of the Philippines. Other important islands include Mindoro, Masbate, Samar, and Cebu. The coastline of the Philippines is 10,850 miles long!

Many of the mountainous islands are really volcanoes. Mount Pinatubo, fifty-five miles northwest of the capital city of Manila, erupted in 1991 for the first time in 600 years, causing more than 700 deaths. A column of ash and smoke rose over nineteen miles high, making Pinatubo perhaps the largest volcanic eruption of the twentieth century.

The city of Manila is no stranger to catastrophe, either; it was flattened during the fighting in the Second World War. The Philippines were the scene of some of the worst combat of the war. First the Japanese armies overran the American positions, forcing the prisoners to make the infamous Bataan Death March, in which many died. When General Douglas MacArthur left the islands, he vowed, "I shall return!" And he did, as American forces eventually triumphed.

Most of the people of the Philippines are of Malay stock. Chinese traders are known to have visited and resided on the islands from about A.D. 1000, but the influence of both China and India on the Philippines was of little importance. The European explorer Ferdinand Magellan landed in the islands on his attempt to sail around the world in 1521. His ship made it, but Magellan himself died at the hands of the fierce natives. Spain did manage to colonize the islands, naming them the Philippines after the Spanish king Philip II.

The United States claimed the islands after its victory in the Spanish-American War of 1898, then lost them to the Japanese during the Second World War. After the Philippines' liberation by U.S. forces in 1944 and 1945, the independent Republic of the Philippines was proclaimed on July 4, 1946. Its government was patterned on that of the United States.

Ferdinand E. Marcos was the first elected president in the 1960s, and in 1972 he declared martial law. The assassination of opposition leader Benigno S. Aquino, Jr., in 1983 became the focal point of mounting opposition to Marcos's increasingly corrupt rule, and he fled to Hawaii when a bloodless revolt drove him from power in 1986. Corazon Aquino, Benigno's widow, took over as president, presiding over a new constitution written in 1987, ushering in a new era of democratic government.

Other Facts About the Philippines

- The Sulu Sea is surrounded by islands in the Philippines chain and the island of Borneo to the south.

- Mount Apo, at 9,692 feet, is the highest peak in the Philippines, overlooking Davao, Mindanao's largest city.

- Typhoons frequently strike the more northerly eastern coast.

- There are many valuable hardwoods, such as lauan (Philippine mahogany) and kapok, as well as many softwoods, including pine. Native plants and animals include some 800 species of orchid and at least 56 species of bat.

- The Philippines calls its currency pesos.

- Important foods in the Philippines include rice, coconuts, cassava, and bananas.

- The two official languages of the Philippines are English and Pilipino, a form of Tagalog that twenty-five percent of the population speaks as a primary language.

- A significant minority in the Philippines are the Moros, who live in the south and are predominantly Muslim. They were never subdued by the Spanish, and many Moros still hope for independence from the Philippine government in Manila.

- Banaue, located on the northern portion of the island of Luzon in the Ifugao province, is famous for its rice terraces. The Ifugao people have been cultivating rice on these terraces for over 2,000 years.

RUSSIA

Where can you cross eleven time zones and still be in the same country? Only in Russia, the world's largest country, and that's not even counting the other fifteen now-independent countries that made up the former Soviet Union. In fact, Russia covers nearly twice the territory of the United States and spans two continents! Russia is so vast that part of it lies in Europe and part of it lies in Asia.

The Ural Mountains form the border between European Russia and Asian Russia. They stretch for 2,500 miles, and are one of the richest mineral-bearing areas in the world. More than 1,000 types of minerals are known to occur, many of which were first discovered there, such as uralite. A thriving steel industry has grown up around the large iron-ore deposits. The Caucasus Mountains lie on the border between the countries of Georgia and Azerbaijan (two of the so-called Caucasian republics), and Russia.

European Russia is mostly a flat area between the two mountain ranges. The Volga River is located there. It is the European continent's longest, flowing 2,193 miles from the mountains north of Moscow all the way to the Caspian Sea. Much of Russia's population lives along its long and winding banks. Lake Ladoga, about 25 miles east of St. Petersburg, is the largest lake in Europe, and has 660 islands in it.

The Asian part of Russia is made up of the plains and plateaus known as Siberia. In fact, most of Russia is in Siberia. Because of its brutally cold climate—some parts of Siberia are even colder in the winter than the North Pole!—it is scarcely populated. Many political prisoners were sent to Siberia under the former communist regime. If you get sent to Siberia nowadays, it may be because of its enormous mineral resources: coal, petroleum, natural gas, diamonds, iron ore, and gold.

Lake Baikal, located in southern Siberia, is the deepest continental body of water on Earth, having a maximum depth of 5,314 feet. It contains about one fifth of the fresh water on Earth's surface. Into Lake Baikal flow 336 rivers and streams. Siberia has over 53,000 rivers that provide eighty percent of Russia's hydroelectric power. Farther east, in the Bering Sea, lies the Kamchatka Peninsula. If you find yourself on the Kamchatka Peninsula in eastern Siberia in winter, you might enjoy the many geysers, hot springs, and twenty-two active volcanoes. The Bering Sea to the far east of Russia separates the continents of Asia (northeastern Siberia) and North America (Alaska). The U.S.-Russian boundary passes right through it.

For many centuries Russia was ruled by emperors, or czars (the Russian word for caesar). The first official czar was Ivan the

Terrible, in the 1500s. Peter the Great (1689–1725) was fascinated with the cultures of Europe, and moved his capital from Moscow to St. Petersburg in order to be closer to Europe. At the beginning of Peter's reign, the Russian empire had no access to the Black Sea, the Caspian, or the Baltic, and the main goal of Peter's foreign policy became to win such an outlet. His granddaughter Catherine the Great extended the empire. She did this mostly at the expense of masses of peasants, or serfs, who were forced to work harder than ever, and probably didn't think Catherine was all that great. (Everyone would probably agree, however, that Ivan the Terrible truly was terrible, after his brutal reign.)

But while the czars relaxed in their Winter Palace, eating little fish eggs (otherwise known as caviar), the Russian people produced some world-famous writers—in particular Leo Tolstoy, Fyodor Dostoyevsky, and Anton Chekhov—as well as famous composers and musicians like Peter Ilich Tchaikovsky, Sergey Rachmaninoff, Aleksandr Borodin, Aleksandr Scriabin, Nikolay Andreyevich Rimsky-Korsakov, Sergey Prokofiev, and Dmitry Shostakovich. The Bolshoi ("Great") Ballet is the leading ballet company of Russia, founded in 1825. The Bolshoi is famous for elaborately staged productions of the classics and children's ballets that preserve the traditions of nineteenth-century classical dance.

Russia's vast landscape has protected it from two attempts at conquest. Both Napoleon and Adolf Hitler sent huge armies to conquer Russia. Both were turned back by the distances they had to cross, especially during the harsh Russian winters.

Russia became the first country to experiment with the socialist ideas of Karl Marx, when Vladimir Lenin came to power during the Russian Revolution in 1917. This form of government was called communist in the West. Karl Marx's claim was that the end result of the revolution would be a state where the rule would be, "From each according to his abilities, to each according to his needs." What the Russians had was more of a dictatorship than a true communist state. When Lenin died in 1924, he was succeeded by the ruthless Joseph Stalin. Stalin really made the Union of Soviet Socialist Republics (U.S.S.R., or Soviet Union) a powerful industrial nation.

The Soviet Union, under Stalin, joined the Allied forces that opposed the Axis powers, led by Adolf Hitler's Germany, during the Second World War. Over twenty million Soviet citizens are said to have been casualties of that war. Stalin was able to keep himself in power by exiling his opponents or killing them. From the 1930s to the 1950s, the Soviet Union was the site of mass murders and mass exiles to work camps. These tactics resulted in millions of deaths.

Russia, as part of the Union of Soviet Socialist Republics, grew into a world power after the Second World War, and for many tense years a rivalry existed between Russia and the United States. It was called the Cold War because the rivalry was never openly displayed. Both countries possessed nuclear capabilities; both countries were major industrial powers. In Russia the nation's industrial accomplishments and military might were celebrated every May Day (May 1), when huge displays of missiles and other weapons were paraded through Moscow's Red Square.

Beginning in the late 1980s, the republics that formed the Soviet Union claimed their independence. Russia's then leader, Mikhail Gorbachev, broke from previous communist rulers and offered friendship to the countries of the West. The Soviet Union officially dissolved in 1991, one day after Gorbachev resigned. The Soviet flag, bearing the hammer and sickle, that flew over the Kremlin (the collection of buildings where Russia's leaders meet to pass laws and debate policies) was lowered.

Political unrest and economic problems still exist in Russia. Hopefully they will have enough beets to make borscht (a famous soup), and vodka to warm their blood, through the long Russian winters.

Other Facts About Russia

- Over the broad, rolling terrain of the steppes in southern Russia roamed the daring horsemen known as Cossacks.

- Even though the port of Murmansk is 125 miles north of the Arctic Circle, its harbor never freezes over, so from December to May it replaces icebound St. Petersburg as Russia's major port of the northwest. Murmansk, whose name means "edge of the Earth," has one of the largest fish-processing plants in Europe.

- The city of Omsk in west-central Russia was once the headquarters of the Siberian Cossacks, and is now an important railroad stop along the Trans-Siberian Express.

- The finest concert hall in Moscow is the Tchaikovsky Concert Hall, named after the world-famous Russian composer.

- The Russian version of the United States' CIA is called the KGB, and many suspense novels are set in the Cold War era of rivalry between the two spy agencies.

- The old Russian capital city of St. Petersburg is situated on the Baltic Sea, which has the dubious distinction of being the largest expanse of brackish water in the world. St. Petersburg was founded by Peter the Great and sprawls across twelve islands.

- The Russian currency is known as rubles. Silver coins called rubles were in use as far back as the thirteenth century.

- Russians claim that the road bridge across the Volga at Saratov, opened in 1965, is the largest in Europe.

- Irkutsk, near Lake Baikal, is one of the major industrial cities of Siberia.

- The Russian author Boris Pasternak won the Nobel Prize in 1958 for his novel *Dr. Zhivago*, but was still persecuted by the communist regime. Though the novel became an international bestseller, it was circulated only in secrecy in his own land.

- The Russian alphabet uses Cyrillic letters. Many are similar to Roman letters, but some are quite different. In Cyrillic, for instance, the Roman *R* is printed backward and sounds like our letter *y*. This alphabet was created by Christian missionaries in the tenth century.

SAUDI ARABIA

*S*alam aleikum ("Peace be with you") and welcome to Saudi Arabia. Go ahead, park your camel near the palm tree at the wadi. (A wadi is a stream that is normally dry, except in the rainy season.) If you travel across this land using a camel, you'll be grateful for its capacity to store water.

The largest nation on the Middle Eastern peninsula, Saudi Arabia is also the largest OPEC nation, known for its immense reserves of oil. It lies between the Red Sea and the Persian Gulf. Most of the land is plateaus, although there are some highlands, like the Hejaz and the Asir, and the Tuwayq Mountains. In the southeastern corner is the Rub al-Khali, the greatest continuous expanse of sand in the world. Rub al-Khali means "empty quarter." The King Fahd Causeway lies between the small islands of Bahrain (a nation in the Persian Gulf) and Saudi Arabia.

Saudi Arabia is so hot and dry that there are no rivers or permanent bodies of water in the country. Consequently, it is the world's largest producer of desalinated water. To desalinate means to desalt, or remove the salt from, seawater.

The two holiest cities of Islam, Mecca and Medina, are found in Saudi Arabia. Medina is where the Prophet's Mosque can be found. Mecca, the holiest city of Islam, is the birthplace of Muhammad, the prophet of Islam. He was born in the year A.D. 570. Most Saudis are Muslim Arabs. According to Islamic teachings, every Muslim should make a pilgrimage to Mecca at least once in his or her life. Non-Muslims are not permitted in the mosque at Mecca. Arabia, for centuries composed of different tribes and groups, was united for the first time under Muhammad. Arabia fell apart, though, after the Arabs spread out and conquered much of the Near East and North Africa.

Later, Arabia was ruled by the Turks, until the 1900s. Abdul Aziz ibn Saud, founder of the Saud dynasty, was able to defeat the Turks. He took over the Hejaz province at that time. The Hejaz railroad ran between Damascus, in modern-day Syria, and Medina. Even before the First World War, the Bedouins of the nearby deserts attacked the railway. T. E. Lawrence, an Englishman who was dedicated to helping the cause of a united and strong Arabia, helped blow up the Hejaz Railroad in 1916. He was known as Lawrence of Arabia.

Oil was discovered in 1938 at the city of Ad-Dammam, on the Persian Gulf, northwest of Bahrain Island. The discovery of immense oil reserves there transformed the small settlement of Ad-Dammam into a major seaport and a petroleum and natural gas center.

The Saudi royal family still rules Saudi Arabia. King Fahd ibn Abdul Aziz is the son of Abdul. The monarchy today has over 6,000 members. That would be one huge family reunion!

Oil has brought great wealth to the country. It is also known for its crops of dates, wheat, barley, and fruits. Arabian horses are some of the finest in the world, and are prized.

Other Facts About Saudi Arabia

- Riyadh, the capital of Saudi Arabia, was chosen as the capital of the Saud dynasty in 1824. It is today the center of commerce, education, and transportation in the kingdom.

- Jeddah is a port city on the Red Sea, not far from Mecca. It is famous for its Corniche—a seaside walkway. The Red Sea is known for its colorful fish and beautiful coral.

- Al-Hufuf is a city near the Persian Gulf. It is known for its Thursday market and as the home of the royal horse-breeding stables. Al-Hufuf was originally the headquarters of the Ottoman government in Arabia.

- Ta'if, once the seat of the pagan goddess Allat, is now sacred as the site of the tomb of 'Abd Allah ibn 'Abbas, a cousin of the prophet Muhammad. There are also two graves there, of two infant sons of the prophet. The king has a summer palace near Ta'if.

- Al Hudaydah, in Yemen, was owned by Saudi Arabia in 1934, but was given back to Yemen in that same year under the terms of the Treaty of At-Ta'if. This treaty cemented the borders between Saudi Arabia and Yemen.

- Tabuk is an oasis town, situated amid a grove of date palms. Near the edge of the old part of town is a Turkish fort, built in 1694.

- Saudis spend riyals to buy frankincense, an aromatic gum resin that is used in incense. Even in ancient times, the scented resin was highly prized and used for medicinal purposes.

- The Saudis are nearly as crazy about soccer as are the Europeans.

- Shwarma is one food you may find a lot of in Saudi Arabia—it's a lamb sandwich, much like Greek gyros or souvlaki.

- The Al Hasa oasis is the largest in Saudi Arabia. It has about 30,000 acres of palm groves and other crops. The flow of sixty or more artesian springs irrigates the oasis. The areas north and west of the oasis are the major oil-producing regions in Saudi Arabia.

- The Najd region of Saudi Arabia is mostly a rocky plateau that slopes eastward from the Hejaz highlands. It is bordered by the sand deserts of an-Nafud, ad-Dahna, and the Rub al-Khali.

- Fifty miles east of the Red Sea, the city of Abha lies at the western edge of Mount al-Hijaz. The valley of the Wadi Abha nearby is filled with gardens, fields, and streams.

SINGAPORE

hat nation is both the smallest country in Southeast Asia and the busiest port in the world? Singapore, which is the name of the city, the country, and the largest island in the country! What once was a fishing village in the mangrove swamps on the tip of the Malay Peninsula is now a prosperous island nation filled with skyscrapers. Singapore specializes in international banking and high-tech electronics.

Singapore Island originally was inhabited by fishermen and pirates, and was called Temasek, from the Javanese word tasek ("sea"). There are fifty-five other islands besides Singapore. The Strait of Malacca, which separates Singapore from the island of Sumatra, is the shortest sea route between India and China and therefore is one of the most heavily traveled shipping channels in the world.

Singapore's location, where the Indian Ocean and the South China Sea meet, has made it a strategic one for European traders. The Portuguese arrived in the sixteenth century, followed by the Dutch and finally the English. In 1819 Sir Thomas

Stamford Raffles of the British East India Company established Singapore as the center of British affairs in the area. He was ultimately rewarded by having the world-famous Raffles Hotel named after him.

Singapore's port area is one of the world's largest. Sembawang, Pasir Panjang, and Telok Ayer are the names of some of the wharves that provide facilities for small vessels all the way up to oceangoing liners.

The name Singapore means "lion city," but since there are no lions on the island, or anywhere in Asia for that matter, no one knows why. According to one account, an Indian prince is said to have glimpsed a tiger there and mistaken it for a lion.

The people of Singapore pride themselves on their modern, clean city. Even if you could find some chewing gum, which isn't sold in Singapore, you'd better watch where you put it—it's a crime to throw it on the ground. Crime is taken very seriously in Singapore. A common punishment for breaking laws is caning, in which the offender is swatted with a stiff cane on bare flesh by a trained martial artist.

Other Facts About Singapore

- The largest English-speaking newspaper in Southeast Asia is the *Straits Times*, published in Singapore.

- Singapore, reflecting its international flavor, has four official languages: English (in which all classes are taught), Mandarin Chinese, Malay, and Tamil.

- The author James Clavell (*Shōgun*) spent three and a half years in the infamous Changi prison camp near Singapore, which was so brutal that only 10,000 of its 150,000 inmates survived. Now Changi is the site of the new international airport.

- Singapore is a great place to eat. If you're adventurous, you might want to try some spicy noodles or crab with chili sauce; or just relax on the beach with some coconut and papaya.

- Don't look for any American presidents on the Singapore dollar—you're more likely to find Chinese characters on it.

- Nearly two thirds of Singapore's landscape lies at less than 50 feet above sea level. Its highest peak, Timah Hill, rises to only 541 feet.

- The growth rate of Singapore's population declined by more than half between the 1960s and 1980 following the introduction of birth-control measures. As a result, less than one fourth of the population is under fifteen years of age.

- Singapore's population is virtually all urban; some eighty-five percent of the people live on twenty-eight square miles, mostly in multistory apartment buildings covering only a few square miles.

- The gross national product (GNP) per capita is the highest in Southeast Asia.

- Singapore manufactures drilling equipment and rigs for offshore oil exploration throughout Asia and is one of the world's leading refiners of petroleum.

- The industrial complex at Jurong, the largest in Southeast Asia, has more than 1,600 factories and manufactures textiles, plywood and veneer, bricks, cement, various chemicals and plastics, steel rods and pipes, and ships. Most manufactures are exported.

- Singapore has more than 100 commercial banks, most of which are foreign.

- In domestic as in international politics, the country's dominant voice for the three decades after independence has been that of its first prime minister, Lee Kuan Yew.

- Feel like taking in a game of cricket? Visit the Singapore Cricket Club located on the Padang ("field") in the heart of downtown Singapore.

- While visiting the Padang, take a look at the Merlion statue. Half fish, half lion, the Merlion is the symbol of Singapore.

- Orchard Road is called the "Oxford Street of Singapore" because of the number of retail stores located there.

SOUTH AFRICA

outh Africa is the country that sits at the very bottom of the African continent. South African geography is largely dominated by the Great Escarpment, the plateau edge that separates the region's interior highlands from the fairly narrow coastal strip. The Great Escarpment lies mainly within the Republic of South Africa and Lesotho but extends northeastward into eastern Zimbabwe (where it separates much of that country from Mozambique) and northwestward into Namibia and Angola (where it separates the central plateaus of those countries from their arid coastal plains).

Much of the Kalahari Desert, in the northern region of South Africa bordering the Namib Desert of Namibia, actually receives quite a bit of rainfall. It probably wouldn't deserve the name desert except for the fact that the water drains right through the sand, leaving no standing sources of water!

Oh, and by the way—make sure you bring plenty of water when you visit the Great Karoo plateau in Western Cape province, because the name means "land of thirst."

The longest river in South Africa is the Orange River, named by early Dutch explorers in honor of the royal Dutch House of Orange. The Crocodile River in the Witwatersrand eventually becomes the Limpopo River and flows northeast and then east for about 1,100 miles all the way to the Indian Ocean. The first European to visit the river was Vasco da Gama, who anchored off its mouth in 1498.

South Africa was colonized by the Dutch and the British, although many people were already living there. In 1652, when the Dutchman Jan van Riebeeck established a colony at the Cape of Good Hope, the native population were primarily nomadic Bushmen (or San), and the Khoi, also called Hottentots. Their way of life had not changed much for thousands of years. Only a century or two before the arrival of the Europeans, Bantu-speaking peoples had begun to migrate southward. They came to South Africa's rolling grasslands and savannas, called the veld by the Europeans.

As more and more European traders began to sail around Africa's southern tip to trade with Asia, many began to settle in South Africa. Dutch settlers in particular came, and were eventually called Boers or Afrikaners, after their Afrikaans language, a mix of Dutch and various native African languages. As the Boers moved farther and farther inland, they began to intrude upon the lands of such peoples as the Xhosa and Zulu, setting off frontier wars that lasted 100 years. In the early nineteenth century the British captured the coastal areas around the Cape of Good Hope, and in the 1830s the Boers sought to escape British rule by embarking upon the Great Trek. This journey led them inland across the Orange and the Vaal rivers. The Boers hauled their covered wagons across the veld much like the American pioneers were doing at the same time in the American West.

Another similarity between the Boers and the American pioneers is that the new settlers in South Africa prevailed in their conflicts with the native peoples through their superior weaponry, primarily muskets. The discovery of diamonds (1868) and gold (1886) near the Boer city of Johannesburg caused the economy to boom during the late nineteenth century. These discoveries also attracted the attention of the British, who defeated the Boers in 1902 and claimed control of all the territories that now make up the country of South Africa.

For hundreds of years, South Africa has faced many challenges. The modern history of South Africa is the story of how different peoples—Boers, English, various black tribal groups—have attempted to share this rich land. Though black Africans make up three fourths of the country's total population, until recently they had never had a voice in the government. The Afrikaners, who outnumbered the English, eventually claimed the leading voice in government. In 1948 the Afrikaners instituted a rigid set of rules, called apartheid, that denied the black majority voting rights and kept them strictly segregated.

Through many struggles and uprisings, led by such people as Bishop Desmond Tutu and Nelson Mandela, the system of apartheid was overturned by 1994, and full voting rights were won for all. Bishop Tutu won the Nobel Peace Prize for his efforts, as did Nelson Mandela, who had spent over twenty years in prison as a political prisoner of the former regime. Mandela was later elected president of South Africa.

One of President Mandela's greatest challenges is how to bring all the different peoples of South Africa into one government. The black population includes various Xhosa, Zulu, Swazi, and Ndebele peoples, whose main languages are Nguni, Sotho,

Tsonga, and Venda. In addition to the English and Afrikaners, the city of Durban, on the Indian Ocean, has the largest Indian population outside of India.

South Africa today is an economic giant. It is the world's largest producer of gold. Some South African gold mines reach depths of over two miles, making them far and away the deepest mines in the world. Although South Africa is also richly endowed with such wealth as diamonds, chromium, and platinum, its real riches lie within the diversity of its peoples. The blending of European and African cultures produces new forms of music, art, dance, and literature.

Other Facts About South Africa

- Cape Town is the legislative capital of South Africa. It is located in one of the world's most scenic natural settings. Much of the city winds about the steep slopes of Table Mountain and its neighboring peaks.

- Cape Agulhas is the southernmost point of the African continent, located 109 miles southeast of Cape Town. Its name, which in Portuguese means "needles," refers to the rocks and reefs that have wrecked many ships.

- The small province of Gauteng contains enormous concentrations of gold, mainly in the ridge of gold-bearing rock in the south known as the Witwatersrand, where Johannesburg is located. The mining, industrial, commercial, and financial activities arising from this vast mineral wealth have made Gauteng the economic hub of South Africa. It is also the most densely populated province.

- Pretoria, the nation's administrative capital, is a well-planned city famous for its streets lined with jacaranda trees. In Pretoria you'll find the Voortrekker Monument, commemorating the Great Trek made by the Boers in the 1830s to escape British rule.

- The luxurious resort city of Sun City, in Bophuthatswana, is South Africa's answer to Las Vegas. Many entertainers from around the world refused to perform there until the apartheid system of government was replaced and the nation's blacks were allowed basic civil rights and a voice in their government.

- It's common in KwaZulu for people to live in a kraal, which consists of a number of huts arranged in a circle around a cattle corral.

- The apartheid government of South Africa created separate areas, which it called homelands, as a way of keeping the black population separate. In 1959 Transkei was created as a homeland for the Xhosa people in the eastern region.

- Bloemfontein ("Fountain of Flowers") is known for its natural and man-made beauties, including the 300-acre King's Park and the Franklin Game Reserve. It's also the judicial capital of South Africa, the home of the National Court of Appeals.

- Paul Kruger was an important leader of the Boers during their period of independence. The town of Krugersdorp, the gold coin known as the Krugerrand, and Kruger National Park, a wildlife reserve with lions, elephants, rhinoceroses, and antelopes, all bear his name.

- When the Portuguese navigator Bartholomeu Dias sailed around the southern tip of the country in 1488, he named it the Cape of Storms. No doubt it was a more optimistic person who later renamed it the Cape of Good Hope!

- De Beers Consolidated Mines, Ltd., is the world's largest producer and distributor of diamonds. Diamonds were first discovered in the mid-1860s on the farm of Nicolaas and Diederick de Beer, near what is now the city of Kimberley. Two diamond mines dug on the farm, the Kimberley and the De Beers, were at one time the world's most productive, though they are no longer in operation.

- The National Botanic Gardens of South Africa, in Cape Province, are one of the world's largest botanical gardens. The 6,200-species collection consists almost exclusively of plants native to southern Africa, and includes such beautiful flowering plants as the protea, South Africa's national flower.

- The KwaZulu city of Pietermaritzburg is known as the City of Flowers for its azaleas, roses, and botanical gardens. The Boers, who founded it in 1839 after a victory over the Zulus at Blood River, named it to honor their dead leaders Piet Retief and Gerrit Maritz.

- The South African rand is the nation's currency. The Krugerrand, a solid-gold coin, is popular among coin collectors, but many nations banned its importation until apartheid was ended.

- The province of Natal was renamed KwaZulu after apartheid ended in 1994, and is the homeland of the Zulu people. The local Zulu name for the eastern face of the Drakensberg range of mountains is Quathlamba, meaning "barrier of pointed spears"—it's an area of many game reserves, scenic national parks, and caves with ancient San (Bushman) paintings and engravings.

- Port Elizabeth was established in 1820 as a British settlement around Fort Frederick (1799), the oldest British building in southern Africa, and was named by Sir Rufane Donkin, the acting governor of the Cape Colony, for his deceased wife, Lady Elizabeth.

SOUTH KOREA

If Japan is the Land of the Rising Sun, then where might the Land of the Morning Calm be? It's South Korea, just west of Japan. It's on the peninsula that juts into the Sea of Japan, from the Chinese province of Manchuria.

Officially, South Korea is known as the Republic of Korea, distinguishing it from its sister country, North Korea (officially called the Democratic People's Republic of Korea). The Korean people live in both countries, but the styles of government are very different.

South Korea is mostly mountainous. The Taebaek Mountains, source of South Korea's major rivers, account for three fourths of the country. They are on the eastern side of the country, on the Sea of Japan, and rise high above the coastal lowlands, where rice is intensively grown. The longest river in South Korea is the Naktong. The Sobaek Mountains form the central region of South Korea.

Mount Halla, an extinct volcano with a crater lake, is the highest point of the country, at 6,398 feet. It's actually on Cheju Island, which belongs to South Korea. Although there are many islands along the southern coasts of South Korea, Cheju is the largest offshore island owned by either Korea.

Although South Korea is smaller than North Korea, its population is nearly twice as large. The two countries were not always separate. The Korean peninsula has long been prized by such foreign invaders as Mongols, Russians, and Japanese. The Yi Dynasty was established in 1392, and during its long reign Korea was greatly influenced by Chinese culture. (China conquered the country in the 1600s.) The Koreans adopted Buddhism and developed a written language similar to Chinese characters, called Hangul. The Yi Dynasty lasted all the way until 1910, when the Japanese annexed Korea.

South Korea actually dates from the Japanese surrender at the end of the Second World War, when Korea was divided into two zones at the Thirty-eighth Parallel. The then Soviet Union occupied the northern part, while the United States controlled the southern part. On June 25, 1950, North Korean troops invaded South Korea, starting the Korean War. United Nations forces, mostly from the United States, intervened on the side of South Korea; Chinese troops intervened on the side of North Korea.

The Korean War lasted for three years and ended without a decisive winner. Since then, both countries have kept to their respective sides of the Thirty-eighth Parallel, staring at each other across a narrow strip of land called the Demilitarized Zone (DMZ). Forty years later, there is still hostility and suspicion between North Korea and South Korea.

Since the war, South Korea has transformed itself into one of the world's most highly industrialized nations. This is a phenomenon, considering that South Korea's economy was nearly destroyed by the Second World War. The capital city of Seoul blooms with cherry blossoms and lotus trees in the springtime, and was the site of the 1988 Olympic games. One fourth of the population of South Korea lives in Seoul. It is one of the largest cities in the world.

One of South Korea's most important modern leaders was General Park Chung Hee, who introduced the "New Community" movement.

General Park's eighteen-year rule brought about enormous economic expansion at the cost of civil liberties and political freedom. He organized and expanded the dreaded Korean Central Intelligence Agency (KCIA), claiming that all his measures were necessary to fight communism. Park grew increasingly harsh toward political dissidents, and after he dismissed a popular opposition leader, Korea erupted into riots and demonstrations. He was eventually assassinated by his lifelong friend Kim Jae Kyu, the head of the KCIA, and South Korea has since moved toward democratic reforms.

Many of the people of South Korea still live in traditional houses with paper walls, which are heated by sending the hot smoke from their wood-burning ovens through pipes running under the floor. Most of the people are Buddhist, but are also strongly influenced by Confucianism, which teaches respect for elders. A sixtieth-birthday party, called a hwan'gap, is a very important occasion in South Korea.

The Koreans, like the Chinese, are big fans of ginseng, and Korean ginseng is now exported all over the world. This root has been widely used in Asian medicine, and is now popular in the West.

A Korean culinary specialty is kimchi, a pickled vegetable relish always served with a Korean meal. Celery, cabbage, Chinese turnips, and cucumbers are sliced, highly seasoned with red pepper, onion, and garlic, and then fermented in brine underground in large earthenware jars for at least a month. Dried and salted shrimp, anchovy paste, and oysters are sometimes used as additional seasonings. Yum!

Other Facts About South Korea

- Tae kwon do is a modern Korean form of martial arts, with lots of high jump kicks and punches, and is practiced for sport, self-defense, and spiritual development.

- The city of Panmunjom was the site in 1994 for talks between North and South Korea to keep the peninsula free of nuclear weapons.

- South Korean money is called won, and the flag has the Korean version of the circular yin-yang symbol, called a taeguk.

- The Korean alphabet is made up of Hangul characters. There are 24 letters.

- Pusan, at the southeast tip of the Korean peninsula, is the nation's largest port and second-largest city. Its name means "kettle mountain," after the shape of the mountain behind it.

- The city of Ulsan, forty-five miles north of Pusan, is the heart of the country's special industrial area known as the Ulsan Industrial District.

- The city of Suwon, twenty-six miles north of Seoul, is a place where visitors can still see how Koreans have traditionally lived for centuries.

- During the Korean War, American Marines made a dramatic landing at the beach of Inchon. Now, many Koreans go there to relax and to swim in the Yellow Sea.

- The Russian port of Vladivostok is across the Sea of Japan from the beaches of Kangnung.

- Since 1234, Koreans have been using movable metal type to publish books on medicine, astronomy, geography, history, and agriculture.

- There is a long tradition of Buddhism in South Korea, as can be seen by such ancient temples as the Pulguk-sa in Kwangju.

- The ancient city of Kwangju dates from the time of the Three Kingdoms, in 57 B.C. It has the world's oldest astronomic observatory, built in A.D. 634.

- Feel like some tasty Korean barbecued meat? Order bulgogi ("fire beef")—it's marinated in soy sauce, sesame oil, garlic, and other seasonings, then cooked over a hot charcoal grill at your table.

SPAIN

This is the land of the Basques in the north and the Gypsies in the south. It is the crossroads between Europe and Africa; a country with a rich history of artistic expression and diverse cultural influences. One of Europe's largest countries, Spain occupies about eighty-five percent of the Iberian Peninsula; Portugal occupies the rest. Spain is bordered on the west by Portugal and the Atlantic Ocean. To the south and east is the Mediterranean, and to the north are the Bay of Biscay and France.

The earliest human residents of Spain lived at least 35,000 years ago. Over the millennia, Spain has been influenced by many cultures, including the Celts, the Greeks and Phoenicians, and the ancient Romans. Great aqueducts built by the Romans still exist in parts of Spain. Another significant influence in Spanish architecture and culture came from an influx of Muslims from North Africa, who at one time controlled the area in the south of Spain called Andalusia. In cities such as Sevilla, Granada, and Córdoba, you can still see magnificent examples of Moorish architecture. One of the greatest examples is the Alhambra, a great fortress built between 1238 and 1358 near the city of Granada.

Spain was once a great colonizing and exploring nation. It was Queen Isabella of Spain who financed Christopher Columbus on his famous voyage to the Indies that resulted in the discovery of America. The Spanish were the first Europeans to establish permanent colonies in the Americas, and their influence still remains, as most countries in Central and South America use Spanish as their official language. It was the Spaniards who were the first in modern times to establish an overseas empire, and Spain was the most powerful country in Europe during the sixteenth and part of the seventeenth centuries.

Today, Spain is primarily democratic. Like the United Kingdom, Spain is technically a monarchy, though for many years it was ruled by Generalissimo Francisco Franco as a military dictatorship. When the hereditary king, Juan Carlos, was returned to power upon Franco's death, he instituted reforms to make the government more representative.

Among Spain's most notable customs are the bullfight, the running of the bulls in Pamplona each year, and the art of flamenco dance and music. Flamenco is heavily influenced by Middle Eastern music and represents a blending of European and Middle Eastern scales and tempos.

Spain is famous for its arts, its artists, and its art forms. Spain has produced many great artists, including Diego de Velázquez, El Greco, Francisco Goya, and, in modern times, Salvador Dalí and Pablo Picasso, who was renowned for his abstract artwork and his various "periods," including his Blue Period. Famous examples of Spanish art can be found in the Prado Museum in

Madrid, although for modern art, the Picasso Museum in Barcelona is worth a visit. In addition to its many celebrated artists, Spain has produced some of the greatest art forgers in history. One particular forger became so well known that his forgeries were actually sought out by serious collectors and sold for high prices.

Probably the most prominent architect in Spain was Antoni Gaudí, whose buildings in and around Barcelona still inspire books and attract tourists. Spain has produced such great composers as Isaac Albeniz, Enrique Granados, Manuel de Falla, and Joaquín Rodrigo. Spain is in some ways the cultural center of the guitar, producing great classical instrumentalists such as Andrés Segovia and Narciso Yepes, and flamenco greats like Sabicas, the Romero family, and Paco de Lucia. Spain has also produced great classical musicians (other than guitarists) such as the cellist Pablo Casals and the opera singer Plácido Domingo.

Spain's most famous writer was Miguel Cervantes, who conceived his classic novel, *Don Quixote*, while in jail. Another of Spain's great writers was Federico García Lorca.

Other Facts About Spain

- Andalusia, which was once the domain of the Moors, is a rich agricultural region that produces olive oil, grapes, and wheat. Cattle are also raised on its plains.

- The Andalusian city of Jerez is the birthplace of the drink called sherry. In Spanish, sherry is called jerez.

- Because Spain is on a peninsula surrounded by water, it has many beaches. The most famous is the Costa del Sol ("Coast of the

Sun") in the south of Spain, where many tourists go to vacation each year.

- The Spanish enjoy a variety of unique food dishes. Paella, a rice casserole containing the rare spice saffron, is one of the most distinctive. Other specialties include sangria, a combination of wine and fruit juices, and gazpacho, a cold tomato-based soup.

- In Spain, a tortilla is an omelette, whereas in Mexico, a tortilla is a flat bread made of cornmeal or wheat flour.

- The 1992 Summer Olympics were held in Barcelona, and the Olympic Village is still there.

- Many kinds of fish are caught in the waters in and around Spain, including cold-water fish from the Atlantic and fish from the warmer Mediterranean. In the mountains, people catch trout and other freshwater fish.

- The Basque people live in the Pyrenees Mountains between Spain and France. They are intensely independent and live an agricultural life, farming and raising livestock such as cattle and sheep. The Basques are also very adventurous, and many Basques were among the original Spanish explorers of the New World. The Basque language is unlike other languages, and dates back to before the Romans. Its exact origins are shrouded in mystery, however, and it has been said that if you weren't born speaking the Basque language you'll never be able to learn to speak it properly.

- Although the official language of Spain is Spanish, there are many regional languages that are still spoken. In the northwest is Galicia, where a language much like Portuguese, called Galician, is spoken. Also in the northwest are the Basque people, with their own language. In the northeast is the region called Catalonia, which was once the province of Aragon. In this area they speak Catalán. In the south, in Andalusia, they speak a strongly accented Spanish, but there is also the Gypsy language Calló. The purest spoken Spanish is called Castilian, which is spoken in the capital, Madrid. Castilian is also the form traditionally spoken on Spanish radio and television.

- The city of Toledo is considered very typical of traditional Spanish towns, so much so that it has been made a national monument. Toledo has been famous for centuries for its high-quality steel and its sword makers. The famous painter El Greco lived in Toledo and many of his great works can be seen on display there.

- The Strait of Gibraltar, which is just south of the famous British-owned Rock of Gibraltar, is a narrow strip of water between southern Spain and northern Africa that separates the Atlantic Ocean from the Mediterranean Sea.

- Although most of Spain is located on the Iberian Peninsula, the Spanish also control several islands, including the Balearic Islands (Menorca, Majorca, Ibiza) and the Canary Islands.

- The currency of Spain is the peseta.

SWEDEN

The Kingdom of Sweden lies in the heart of Scandinavia, between Norway to the west and Finland to the east. The city of Helsingborg in southern Sweden lies at the narrowest part of the Öresund ("Sound"), which separates Sweden from Denmark. Helsingborg is the most convenient place for motor traffic to cross to and from the European continent.

The capital city of Stockholm, the "Venice of the North," spreads across many islands. In the center of Stockholm is the Old Town section known as Gamla Stan. The Old Town has many majestic buildings from the sixteenth and seventeenth centuries. Sweden is famous for Swedish meatballs and the delicious feast called smÜrgîsbord (smorgasbord), but there's a lot more than just good eating to discover in this land of forests and fjords.

Many Swedes are descendants of the Vikings, and still enjoy sailing on the Baltic Sea (which is surprisingly warm in the summer because it is so shallow). In the far north of Sweden is the region known as Lapland, where the people called Lapps live.

The Lapps, also called the Saami, traditionally herd reindeer, but radioactive fallout from the nuclear disaster at Chernobyl, in Ukraine, has contaminated the milk and meat, forcing many Lapps to take other jobs. Many of them have become miners or foresters.

Sweden still has a king and queen, but the real power lies with the Riksdaghuset, the democratically elected parliament. There is wide agreement among the people of Sweden that social welfare should be one of the main duties of government. Housing, low-cost medical care, and education are guaranteed to all citizens, whatever their economic status. These benefits are financed by high taxes on personal income.

About fifteen percent of Sweden lies north of the Arctic Circle. There, the sun doesn't set at all in the summer and never rises above the horizon in the winter. For many centuries, Swedes have celebrated St. Lucia's Day, on December 13, just before the darkest time of the year. The ceremony features a "Light Queen" who, wearing a white gown and a crown of lighted candles, represents the returning sun.

The Swedes have lived in present-day Sweden for at least 5,000 years. Gothic tribes from Sweden helped defeat the Roman Empire. They were also responsible for creating the Russian state in the ninth century. The Swedish government became a monarchy, and a parliament was established in the 1400s. It was the earliest parliament in all of Europe.

Although the Swedes were ruled by Danish kings, Gustavus Vasa broke away from Denmark in 1523 and became the ruler of an independent Sweden, establishing a lineage of Vasa kings that lasted until 1720. He also established the Lutheran Church in Sweden. Today, the Evangelical Lutheran Church of Sweden is the state religion, and ninety percent of Swedes are members. Sweden acquired Norway during the Napoleonic Wars, but Norway was granted independence in 1905. Those were the last armed conflicts Sweden ever participated in. Even during the two World Wars, Sweden, like Switzerland, maintained a position of armed neutrality.

Sweden today has a developed market economy that is largely based on services, heavy industries, and international trade. The gross national product (GNP) has grown more rapidly than the population, and the GNP per capita is among the highest in the world. Many immigrants have been welcomed into Sweden in recent times as political unrest in Europe and the Middle East has risen.

Other Facts About Sweden

- The flag of Sweden is blue with a yellow cross.

- The money of Sweden is called kronor.

- The country's official language, Swedish, belongs to the North Germanic language group and is closely related to Norwegian and Danish.

- Of Sweden's 90,000 lakes, Lake Vänern, with an area of 2,156 square miles, is the largest; it is Europe's third-largest lake.

- More than eighty percent of the population lives in cities, and the Stockholm-Göteborg-Malmö triangle in the southern part of the country is quite densely populated.

- Forests cover more than two thirds of the land, and Sweden is a major exporter of forest products, such as prefabricated houses, boards, and furniture.

- Everybody reads in Sweden; the literacy rate is 100 percent.

- The Nobel Prizes, awarded in Stockholm every year, were established by the nineteenth-century Swedish citizen Alfred Nobel, the inventor of dynamite.

- Besides a famous bird sanctuary, Oland Island contains the ruins of one of the finest castles and strongest fortresses in Sweden. Located in Borgholm, it dates from the thirteenth century or before.

- The town and port of Norrköping lies along the Motala River southwest of Stockholm and is known for the Hällristningar, or rock carvings, that are found in the area and date from the Late Bronze Age.

- In 1567 and 1612, the town of Jönköping in southern Sweden was set on fire by its own citizens as Danish armies approached. Today, the leading industry in the city is the manufacture of matches.

- The Lule River provides hydroelectric power for the industries of northern Sweden as it makes its way to Luleå, where it enters the Gulf of Bothnia.

- Göteborg, also spelled Gothenburg, is Sweden's chief seaport and second-largest city.

- The *Vasa* Museet is a museum containing the wrecked remains of the *Vasa*, an old Viking ship.

- Famous Swedes include the tennis player Bjorn Borg, the movie director Ingmar Bergman, and the popular band of the 1970s, ABBA.

- Sweden's highest peak is Mount Kebnekaise at 6,926 feet above sea level.

TANZANIA

The East African nation of Tanzania is a country of dramatic landscapes. From the snowcapped peaks of Africa's highest mountain, Mount Kilimanjaro, you can go to the shores of Africa's biggest lake, Lake Victoria. Or try diving into the depths of the world's second-deepest lake, Lake Tanganyika. The longest freshwater lake in the world, at 410 miles, it forms the boundary between Tanzania and Zaire. It is 4,710 feet deep. Only Lake Baikal in Russia is deeper.

Although three great rivers—the Nile, the Congo, and the Zambezi—have their origins in Tanzania, the country has few rivers that flow all year round and don't dry up periodically. The country's largest river is the Rufiji, which flows east into the Indian Ocean. The Kalambo River, which flows into Lake Tanganyika, has one of the highest waterfalls in the world, at 704 feet.

Tanzania has lots of neighbors: Malawi and Mozambique in the south; Zambia, Zaire, Burundi, and Rwanda in the west; Uganda and Kenya in the north; and the Indian Ocean to the east. Only about four percent of Tanzania's land is suitable for agriculture, so many people, like the Masai, are nomadic cattle herders.

Did you know the gnu, the wildebeest, and the African antelope are all the same animal? If you like wildlife, Tanzania's got plenty: wildebeests, elephants, rhinoceroses, hippopotamuses, buffalos, lions, leopards, zebras, giraffes, elands, kudus, and dik-diks. Tanzania also includes the island of Zanzibar, which has its own kind of leopard, as well about twenty species of bats and thirty kinds of snakes. Serengeti National Park, in north-central Tanzania, is an international tourist attraction best known for its huge herds of plains animals (especially wildebeests, gazelles, and zebras).

The Serengeti game preserve is the only place in Africa where vast land-animal migrations still take place. The killing of elephants for their ivory tusks, the slaughter of the now virtually extinct black rhinoceros for its horn (which is prized in Yemen for dagger handles), and the poaching of game animals for meat are major problems for the park authorities.

Tanzania used to be called Tanganyika, just like the lake. During colonial times, in the 1800s, it was part of German East Africa. Then Great Britain took over during the First World War, and Tanganyika gained its independence in 1961. In 1964, Tanganyika joined with the island of Zanzibar to become a single nation, the United Republic of Tanzania. Zanzibar, called the Island of Cloves, has a separate government.

But the history of the area goes back much further than modern times, or the even more ancient days when the Arabs, the Portuguese, and other Europeans swept through Tanzania. The archaeologists Louis and Mary Leakey were searching through the Great Rift Valley when they discovered, in a place called Olduvai Gorge, the two-million-year-old bones of a human ancestor.

Other Facts About Tanzania

- Tanzania's capital is presently Dar es-Salaam, but since the early 1980s Tanzania has been in the process of moving it to Dodoma, an agricultural center known especially for its peanuts.

- You won't find the Godfather on Mafia Island, in the Indian Ocean off the eastern coast of Tanzania, but the fishing's excellent.

- Tanzania's currency is called shillings.

- Because of the very high birthrate, almost half of Tanzania's population is less than fifteen years old.

- A majority of Tanzania's 120 ethnic groups speak Bantu languages, mostly Swahili, which is one of the country's two official languages. (English is the other.)

- The dreaded tsetse fly, which carries the disease called sleeping sickness, thrives on wild game in miombo woodlands. This makes human settlement hazardous in areas of moderate rainfall. In Tanzania, areas of low or unreliable rainfall are more densely populated than you'd otherwise expect. The insect does not pose a threat to areas of high rainfall and high population density.

- Tanzania has television only on the island of Zanzibar.

- Julius Nyerere, the country's first president, was a literary figure of note, known especially for his translations of Shakespeare's plays into Swahili.

- In 1871 Sir Henry Morton Stanley "found" the famous English explorer David Livingstone at Ujiji.

THAILAND

The Kingdom of Thailand has been called Asia's Land of the Free, because it is the only Southeast Asian country that was never a European colony. It's also the only Southeast Asian country shaped like the head of an elephant!

If you hopped onto a raft on the Mun River, in eastern Thailand, you'd eventually wind up on the Mekong River, which forms the boundary with neighboring Laos, and from there you could go through Cambodia, another neighbor, and Vietnam all the way to the South China Sea. Myanmar (Burma) borders Thailand in the northwest, near the Tanen Mountains. Mount Inthanon, the country's highest peak at 8,481 feet, is located in the Tanen Mountains.

If you had to haul your canoe overland from the Gulf of Thailand to the Andaman Sea, the quickest way would be across the skinny Isthmus of Kra. The isthmus, which borders a narrow part of Burma, connects the main northern areas of Thailand to the southernmost regions and Malaysia. Thailand has many islands, which are located both in the Gulf of Thailand and in the Andaman Sea.

If you've ever seen a Siamese cat, its ancestors probably came from Siam—that's what Thailand used to be called. Of course, cats in Thailand would have to be careful and stay far out of the way of elephants, gibbons, tigers, leopards, wild pigs, pythons, king cobras, and crocodiles.

And cats roaming through the floating markets of the capital city of Bangkok have their paws full just staying out the water: Bangkok's been called the "Venice of the East" because of all the canals that run through it. (Do you suppose that Venice is called the "Bangkok of the West"?) Bangkok is a bustling, crowded city, with Buddhist temples, factories, shops, and homes all interspersed along its roads and canals.

The Thai people call their capital city Krung Thep for short. The full name translates as "The City of Gods, the Great City, the Residence of the Emerald Buddha, the Impregnable City of the God Indra, the Grand Capital of the World Endowed with Nine Precious Gems, the Happy City Abounding in Enormous Royal Palaces Which Resemble the Heavenly Abode Wherein Dwell the Reincarnated Gods, a City Given by Indra and Built by Vishnukarm." Quite a mouthful!

Because Thailand is sixty percent forest, it was known for its exports of teak, a hardwood especially useful for boats and furniture. So much forest was destroyed that commercial logging was banned in 1989, until the land could recover. Today, Thailand is the world's largest exporter of canned pineapple, although some of the largest factories for processing are owned by Japanese companies. Fifty percent of the canned pineapple exported from Thailand goes to the United States. Thailand has been industrializing rapidly, and has many factories where electronic products are made. It is also the leading manufacturer of integrated circuits—the silicon chips found in computers.

In the Golden Triangle, which is the name of the remote northern area where Laos, Thailand, and Myanmar (Burma) meet, growing opium poppies is one of the few sources of income. The Hmong tribesmen have traditionally grown opium poppies as a cash crop. Opium is an ingredient in useful painkilling drugs, as well as highly addictive dangerous drugs like heroin. Governments are urging that other useful or valuable plants be grown in this area instead. One popular alternative to the opium poppy is the orchid.

The Thai people came from southern China from the third to the eleventh centuries. The kingdom was established in the 1300s, with the Thai kings having absolute authority. Although influenced by the west in the 1600s, Thailand remained independent.

Both the walled Grand Palace complex and Bangkok's oldest temple, Wat Po, were built in the early 1800s by one of Thailand's greatest kings, Rama I. The reason Thailand wasn't taken over by European colonial powers was the strong rule of Rama's successors, King Mongkut and his son King Chulalongkorn, who ruled Thailand throughout much of the 1800s. King Chulalongkorn, who reigned until 1910, was responsible for modernizing Thailand and signing trade treaties with France and Britain. Thailand's second-largest city, Nakhon Ratchasima, grew rapidly during the 1960s and 1970s with the buildup of its Royal Thai Air Force Base, from which American planes operated during the Vietnam War.

Thailand is a constitutional monarchy with a parliamentary government that, since 1932, has largely been dominated by the military, which owns most of the radio and many television stations.

With its ancient temples, lovely beaches, and friendly people, Thailand today has become very popular with tourists. If you really want to relax, try the resorts on the island of Phuket, in the Andaman Sea.

Other Facts About Thailand

- Thailand's money is called bahts.

- Thailand's most important mineral resource is tin; its reserves amount to about five percent of the world's total.

- Chaing Mai, in northern Thailand, contains the ruins of many thirteenth- and fourteenth-century temples, called wats, and is famous as a center of Thai handcrafts such as silverwork, wood carving, pottery, umbrellas, and lacquerware.

- Wat Chedi Luang, in Chiang Mai, housed the famous Emerald Buddha during the fifteenth and sixteenth centuries, before the Buddha was moved to Bangkok.

- The city of Nan lies about ninety miles northeast of Lampang along the Nan River, and is a commercial center for teak, bamboo, and rattan products.

- The most important river in Thailand is the Chao Phraya. All of Thailand's capitals, past and present, have been situated on its banks or those of its tributaries.

- Did you know that some bird's nests are edible? If you've ever had one, maybe it was shipped from Songkhla, one of Thailand's major seaports.

- Thailand has a subtropical monsoonal climate with three distinct seasons: the hot season (March–April), the rainy season (May–October), and the cool season (November–February).

- Indigenous minorities include the hill-dwelling Karen, and the Semang, who hunt with blowpipes and spears.

- More than one third of the population is under fifteen years of age.

TURKEY

re you finally ready to talk Turkey? If not, maybe a trip to the Turkish baths would help. Afterward, you might want to try a Turkish coffee, but be careful—they like it strong in Istanbul. Or is it Constantinople—or even Byzantium?

Actually, the most famous city in Turkey (and the only city built on two separate continents!) has been called all three names. Istanbul sits on the Bosporus, the strait that separates Asia Minor from Europe. Likewise, the country of Turkey has a leg in two separate worlds, Asia and Europe. The larger, Asian part of Turkey is called Anatolia. It is separated from the smaller, European part, Thrace, by the Bosporus, the Sea of Marmara, and the Dardanelles Strait. A democratic republic, like Greece, its neighbor to the west, Turkey is overwhelmingly Muslim, like Iran, its neighbor to the east.

Legend has it that the remains of Noah's Ark will one day be found on Mount Ararat, the highest peak in Turkey at 16,853 feet. If you're looking for bulls (or just a Ford), you might try the Taurus Mountains, which rise to the south of the Central Anatolian Plateau. Wild animals include the wolf, fox, boar, wildcat, marten, hyena, bear, deer, and gazelle.

Turkey has been the land of empires: first the Hittites, then the Persians, the Greeks, the Byzantines (for a thousand years!), and finally the Ottomans. The Ottoman Empire ruled vast territories for nearly 400 years. It lasted from the late fifteenth century all the way to the early twentieth, and included the Balkans, Southwest Asia, and North Africa. The Ottoman Empire once stretched from the Red Sea to present-day Hungary, but after the rule of Suleiman the Magnificent (1494–1566), the empire began its long, slow decline. The Ottoman Empire continued to be ruled by sultans until 1918, when it broke up during the First World War. Just before the war, the Ottoman Empire still spanned modern-day Syria, Lebanon, Iraq, Jordan, Israel, Saudi Arabia, Yemen, and islands in the Aegean Sea. Turkey participated in the First World War on the side of Germany and Austria, and lost a lot of territory as a result.

It was in the ancient eastern city of Erzurum, in July 1919, that Mustafa Kemal (later called Ataturk) presided over the first Turkish nationalist congress. Kemal Ataturk, aided by reformers calling themselves the Young Turks, established the present republic in its current capital of Ankara.

Turkey's history has long been intertwined with that of Greece. Troy, the site of the Trojan War made famous by the Greek poet Homer, was excavated in the late nineteenth century. Alexander the Great's armies marched across what was then part of the Persian Empire on their way to India. Even today many Greek temples can be found on Turkish islands in the eastern Aegean Sea. In 1963 Greece and Turkey almost went to war over who owned the island of Cyprus, where both Greeks and Turks have lived for many centuries.

Though Turkey is predominantly Muslim, the emperor Constantine, who founded Constantinople, was a Christian. Constantine built the world-famous basilica called Hagia Sophia. No visitor to the city now known as Istanbul would dream of missing a tour of it.

Kurdish, the native language of nearly twenty percent of the population, is widely spoken by Kurds living near the headwaters of the Tigris and Euphrates rivers. Since the defeat of Iraq in the Gulf War, millions of Kurdish refugees fled Iraq and now live in the border area between Turkey and Iraq.

Other Facts About Turkey

- The Turkish flag is red with a white star and crescent.

- If you're fifteen years old, then forty percent of the Turkish people are your age or younger.

- Turkey is the Middle East's leading steel producer.

- Turkey's money is called lira.

- The "Turquoise Coast" on the Mediterranean Sea, just north of the island of Rhodes, is a favorite destination for sunbathers.

- Don't drink the water of Lake Van, Turkey's largest lake—it's too salty!

- The Persian mystic poet Rumi lived in the central Turkish city of Konya. Rumi's deeply spiritual poems were the inspiration for the Sufi order of Whirling Dervishes, so named for the twirling dance that is their main ritual.

- The modern Black Sea port of Trabzon was one of the eastern-most of ancient Greek settlements, founded in 756 B.C.

- When the weather gets too hot in Cappadocia, go underground! A whole city was built under the ground centuries ago, probably to offer a hiding place in case of attack.

- Adana is Turkey's fourth-largest city, and is the center of Turkey's important cotton industry.

- People have lived in the city of Izmir, one of Turkey's most important seaports, for at least 5,000 years. In ancient times it was known as Smyrna, and was one of the early seats of Christianity.

- Have you noticed that lots of cities in Turkey used to be called something else? The city of Manisa, for instance, was once Magnesia, and even today the mineral magnesite is mined there.

THE UNITED KINGDOM

What do people from England, Scotland, Wales, and Northern Ireland all have in common? Some of them might say, not much! But the fact is, they all live in a land called the United Kingdom. Considering it's such a little group of islands off the coast of Europe, Britain has sent people all over the world, and in many cases they ended up in charge of foreign lands and people. From Australia to Canada to the Middle East to India, the British Empire once stretched so far around the world that it was said the sun never set on it.

The British Isles, considered part of the continent of Europe, are divided into two major islands—Great Britain and Ireland, which lie between the Atlantic Ocean and the North Sea. There are many smaller islands around the main two. England, Wales, and Scotland are all on the same island, Great Britain. The United Kingdom also owns Gibralter, the British West Indies, Bermuda, and islands in the Pacific Ocean, the South Atlantic, and the Indian Ocean. The Channel Islands and the Isle of Man belong to the British crown, but are not considered part of the

United Kingdom. The British ninety-nine-year lease on Hong Kong expires in 1997.

Julius Caesar and the Romans conquered Britain in A.D. 43. They built a city and named it Londinium, now called London. Hot mineral springs are what first brought the Roman invaders to the area, and they ended up founding the city of Bath. After the Romans, the Jutes, Angles, and Saxons came from German lands. The last successful invasion of England was from the Normans, a French-speaking people who came from across the Channel. For a time, England was actually united with parts of France!

But even before all of this, a people known as druids left mysterious monuments to their culture. There are circular rock formations all over the country. The most famous, known as Stonehenge, still puzzles modern-day researchers trying to understand how such huge rocks could have been carried so far, and for what purpose.

England itself is divided into several parts—the northern section has mountains, such as the Cumbrian Mountains and the Pennines. The central or Midlands area is flatter and has farmland and industry. As perhaps befits the home of the Industrial Revolution, farming is highly mechanized. Although three fourths of the land is used for farming, agriculture accounts for less than two percent of the jobs in England. Because of this, England is not self-sufficient and must import food. The southeast is mostly urbanized. In fact, about ninety-two percent of the population in the United Kingdom lives in urban areas.

Scotland, the most northerly part of Great Britain, is the most mountainous. There are many lakes there, called lochs. Ben

Nevis, in Scotland, is the highest point in the United Kingdom, at 4,406 feet.

Northern Ireland, a small part of Ireland, is made up of six of the nine counties of the ancient province of Ulster. Unlike the mostly Catholic southern Ireland, the north was settled by Protestants who came from England and Scotland in the seventeenth century. The larger, southern part declared independence in 1922 and became the Republic of Ireland.

Wales, a small, mountainous area in the west-central area of Great Britain, is known as Cymru (pronounced KUM-ree) in Welsh. The Welsh people are descendants of the Celts, who were driven into the mountains by Anglo-Saxon invaders. Wales has been ruled by England since the late Middle Ages.

England was able to establish its extended colonial empire mostly because it became a naval power early on. Because of England's worldwide empire, the English language is spoken around the world, though the people who speak it don't always approve of how the English behaved. Even the modern-day United States of America began as a British colony and required a war to cut its ties to the British king. If you live in the United States, you might call a certain tune "My Country, 'Tis of Thee," but in England they prefer to think of it as their national anthem and call it "God Save the Queen."

One of England's kings even started his own religion. King Henry VIII, denied a divorce by the Pope, turned his back on the Catholic Church. He founded the Anglican Church in the sixteenth century, and installed the Archbishop of Canterbury as its head. The archbishop promptly granted Henry's request for a divorce, and Henry remarried five times after that. Two of his wives, Anne Boleyn and Katherine Howard, were beheaded on Henry's orders.

Henry VIII's daughter Elizabeth I, called the Virgin Queen, ruled England for nearly fifty years. In 1588 the defeat of the Spanish Armada by England's navies prevented an invasion by Spain, and Brittania would rule the waves for centuries after. During Elizabeth's reign, England became a major naval power and explorers like Sir Francis Drake and Sir Walter Raleigh sailed to new lands and claimed them as British colonies.

The royal family in present-day England is still high profile, but no longer has the power to start churches. The reigning monarch's powers are largely for show; for instance, the right to veto legislative acts has not been exercised since the early eighteenth century. Nowadays the royals are treated more like movie stars, with newspapers and magazines competing to publish intimate stories about their lives. The crown jewels are the royal family's greatest treasure and are kept secure in the Tower of London, not far from the River Thames (pronounced tems).

You might remember the tales of King John (1199–1216) from the legends of Robin Hood. He was the cruel and corrupt ruler who eventually was forced to sign the Magna Carta (1215). The Magna Carta established the constitutional principle that the king must govern according to law and not simply by whim. It was this landmark document that was the beginning of the parliamentary system. The Magna Carta represented the end of power that rested only in the hands of a king or queen.

Today, Parliament consists of two houses: the House of Lords, which is largely advisory, and the House of Commons, which passes most of the laws.

In the parliamentary system, whichever party is elected into power chooses a prime minister. In England, the Prime Minister lives at 10 Downing Street, not far from the royal residence at Buckingham Palace.

Britain was known for its industrial advances throughout the nineteenth and early twentieth centuries. Even though the British won in the First World War, they suffered heavy losses and economic problems. During the Second World War, before the United States entered the conflict, Britain stood almost alone against Germany's forces in the west. France had fallen, and the English, although they were nearly defeated, resisted German air attacks for a full year before they were joined by the Americans. When the Royal Air Force was able to repel the German Luftwaffe in the Battle of Britain, England's prime minister, Winston Churchill, said, "Never in the field of human conflict was so much owed by so many to so few."

In the 1960s, black rhythm-and-blues music from America went to England, where it influenced a generation of bands such as the Beatles and the Rolling Stones. The British bands in turn achieved great popularity by playing their versions of R&B for rock-and-roll audiences in the States.

Even now, although the sun has definitely set on the empire, the United Kingdom can be proud of its heritage. England, for instance, has given us Shakespeare, the parliamentary system, public education, and the Beatles. From Wales have come entertainers like Tom Jones and Anthony Hopkins. Scotland's legacy has included bright tartan kilts, sweet shortbread cookies, and the Loch Ness Monster.

Other Facts About the United Kingdom

- One of the premier Grand Slam tournaments of professional tennis is held in England every summer on Wimbledon's grass courts.

- If you were rich and lived in England, it might be hard to carry all your money around, for British money is called pounds.

- One of the first sights of England that many travelers coming across the Channel from France see are the famous White Cliffs of Dover.

- The professors at two of the United Kingdom's oldest universities, Cambridge and Oxford, are called "dons."

- If you lived near Piccadilly, you wouldn't have very far to run to join the circus—Piccadilly Circus is a famous traffic circle, or roundabout, in London.

- Legend has it that Sir Isaac Newton discovered gravity by having an apple fall on his head, but what was he doing sitting under an apple tree anyway—shouldn't he have been in class?

- Cricket is a popular game in England, played with a ball, bats, and wickets. One game can sometimes go on for several days.

- One of England's most famous novelists was Charles Dickens, who wrote such works as *Great Expectations*, *A Tale of Two Cities*, *Oliver Twist*, *Bleak House*, and even *A Christmas Carol*, complete with Tiny Tim and all those ghosts.

- The British Broadcasting System, or BBC, is one of the finest networks in the world. You can catch it on your TV, or "telly," as they say in England.

- The English call french fries "chips," as in fish and chips. They also call apartments "flats" and elevators "lifts."

- The English town of Yorkshire may be best known for its Yorkshire pudding.

- The Bard, as William Shakespeare is sometimes called, lived in Stratford-upon-Avon. His plays, such as *Hamlet*, *Macbeth*, and

Romeo and Juliet, were first performed at the Globe Theatre in London.

• The ancient tin mines of Cornwall and the iron-ore deposits of north-central England helped to build the Industrial Revolution. Now they are nearly depleted.

• The Scottish capital of Edinburgh is dominated by a magnificent medieval castle. You can visit it from the center of town by walking along the main thoroughfare known as the Royal Mile.

• Clydesdale horses take their name from the land through which the River Clyde flows. The Scottish shipbuilding town of Glasgow sits on the banks of the River Clyde, where it's deep and wide enough for seagoing ships to navigate.

• The most impressive place to be buried in England is in Westminster Abbey, a majestic cathedral.

THE UNITED STATES OF AMERICA

When people say that the United States is a melting pot, they mean that it's a place where people from many different cultures live together to form a single new culture. But nobody really melts; so maybe a better name would be the Great Stew Pot, where everyone adds his or her own separate spice and flavor to the soup. America is a land of immigrants. Every citizen except those of pure Native American descent has roots in other countries. One of the first sights that many immigrants saw as they sailed into New York Harbor was the inspiring Statue of Liberty, a gift to the people of the United States from the people of France.

Just about everything under the sun happens somewhere in the United States. Want to make movies? Try going to Hollywood, out in California. Want to strike it rich on the stock market? Go to Wall Street, in New York City, New York. Want to get all shook up by catching a glimpse of some blue-suede shoes? Go to Graceland, the home of Elvis Presley in Memphis, Tennessee. Want to go to the moon? Well, you'll have to talk to the people at NASA in Houston, Texas—they're the ones who put astronauts into orbit.

The United States is on the North American continent. This continent, as well as South America, was named for the Italian explorer Amerigo Vespucci—although history records that Christopher Columbus landed there first. The United States is the fourth-largest country in the world, with the third-largest population.

Four of the freshwater Great Lakes form part of the boundary between the United States and Canada: Lake Erie, Lake Ontario, Lake Superior, and Lake Huron. Lake Michigan is entirely within U.S. borders.

The border between the United States and Canada is the longest border in the world.

People in the United States call themselves Americans, and they like to give their cities nicknames. New York City is the Big Apple. Los Angeles is sometimes called the City of Angels, and is also known as the Big Orange. Chicago is the Windy City; can you guess why? Detroit is where the automobile industry got its start, so it's called the Motor City. The people of New Orleans enjoy relaxing so much, their city is called the Big Easy. And San Francisco is nicknamed The City, and is also known as the Bay Area, because of the San Francisco Bay.

The United States is a diverse and beautiful nation. It encompasses several major mountain ranges, from the Rockies, Coast Range, and the Sierra Nevada in the west, to the Ozarks in the midwest, to the Allegheny, Catskill, Adirondack, and Smoky Mountains of the east. The Rockies are the most important range in the United States, dividing the country into two regions. Several major rivers, including the Colorado, the Missouri, and the Rio Grande, have their origins in the Rockies. One of the most spectacular sights in the world is the Grand Canyon, which the Colorado River has been carving out of the southwestern landscape for hundreds of millions of years.

The United States also has a number of flatter, open areas between the mountains, like the Great Plains, in the middle of the country. For thousands of miles, farmers can grow crops like wheat and corn in the rich soil.

In the west are deserts like the Mojave and the Sonora. The Mississippi River begins in the Great Plains, as its system drains from the plateaus and plains. The Mississippi–Missouri–Red Rock River is the longest river in the United States.

In the early days, America was explored and settled by Europeans from different countries—England, Spain, France, the Netherlands, and Italy. Florida was first explored by adventurers like the Spaniard Ponce de León, who searched in vain across the endless swamps of the Everglades looking for the fabled Fountain of Youth. One of the first European settlements in the New World, Jamestown, was founded in 1607 on the Chesapeake Bay, the largest bay on the eastern coast of the United States. The Native American heroine Pocahontas was the daughter of a powerful chief, Powhatan. Her brave action in saving the life of Captain John Smith helped ensure peaceful relations for a while between the nearby Potomac Indians and the British colonists in Jamestown.

When Christopher Columbus arrived in America (well, actually the Bahamas), he came by accident. He was trying to sail to India, but didn't realize he'd run into a whole continent first. When his men landed on the shores of the Bahamas and saw brown-skinned natives walking around, they called the native people "Indians," thinking they had landed in India. Today we refer to the first peoples to inhabit this land as Native Americans. The land the European settlers had come to was sometimes called the New World, but of course it wasn't new to the people who were already there.

There are still many Native Americans in the United States. According to the Bureau of Indian Affairs, there were between five million and fifteen million Native Americans in 1492. Today, almost two million Americans in the United States claim Indian ancestry. The Native Americans engaged in and lost many wars with the colonists and the United States government. Many of them were killed in these wars or as a result of war. They also died off because Europeans brought foreign diseases such as smallpox, to which the Indians had no resistance.

Many Indian tribes still pursure their traditional ways of life, living in areas that were set aside by the American government for Native Americans. These areas are called reservations. In the Great Plains, Indians called the Lakota, or Sioux, live. The Iroquois are found in the Northeast. The Hopi live on great mesas in the West. The Navajo people are the only Native Americans who were given back their ancestral lands. The Navajo Nation is in the Southwest.

Today the United States is made up of fifty states. When the United States was born, in 1776, there were only thirteen colonies, all on the east coast. They were possessions of England until they issued the Declaration of Independence, which explained why they wanted freedom from England. In the Declaration, the Founding Fathers said, "We hold these truths to be self-evident, that all men are created equal, that they are endowed by their Creator with certain unalienable Rights, that among these are Life, Liberty, and the pursuit of Happiness." The Revolutionary War began in 1775 and lasted for eight years. There's no food more American than hot dogs and apple pie, and there's no better day to eat them than on the Fourth of July, when the United States celebrates its independence from England.

One of the most painful times in American history was the Civil War, in the mid-1800s. The United States was then split into two parts, the North and the South, and young men from each side fought each other. The Confederate South, rich with cotton and determined to preserve the institution of slavery, split off from the Union.

President Abraham Lincoln was determined to preserve the Union, and delivered a famous speech at the scene of one of the bloodiest battles of the war: Gettysburg, Pennsylvania. He began the speech with the words "Four score and seven years ago," and ended the speech by saying that "government of the people, by the people, and for the people, shall not perish from the earth." Starting in April 1861, the Civil War lasted for four long, bloody years.

The fundamental law of the land in the United States is the Constitution, agreed upon by the Founders in 1791. The Preamble to the Constitution begins with the famous three words "We the People." Originally, only white men could vote, and an amendment to the Constitution had to be written to include black men, too. Eventually it was agreed that all women were created equal as well, and American women were given the right to vote in the 1920s, nearly 150 years after American men!

Today the United States is a world leader in many things, from scientific innovation and military power to rock and roll and blue jeans. The greatest challenge now facing the people of the United States is to lead wisely, so that the many problems facing the world can be solved.

Other Facts About the United States

- The nation's capital is Washington, D.C., where the President lives in the White House, Congress meets under the magnificent dome of the Capitol Building, and the Supreme Court, the highest court in the land, hears its cases.

- The Pentagon, in Arlington, Virginia, is a five-sided building that houses the Department of Defense.

- Why would anyone be so attached to a cracked bell? Well, if it's the Liberty Bell, it's because it rang out in 1776 when the Declaration of Independence was first proclaimed. Ever since, the bell has been a symbol of freedom.

- Many Indian people were upset when the images of four U.S. presidents (Washington, Jefferson, Lincoln, and Teddy Roosevelt) were carved into the face of Mount Rushmore, situated on what the Indians considered sacred land.

- Sometimes the United States is symbolized by the character of Uncle Sam, who has long white hair and chin whiskers and is dressed in a swallow-tailed coat, vest, tall hat, and striped trousers.

- To many people, the theater is not a place you go to watch a movie, but where you go to watch a live play, especially if you're lucky enough to see one on Broadway in New York City.

- It's much easier to float things than to haul them across land. That's why everyone was so happy when the Erie Canal was built, which allowed barges carrying goods from the West to follow waterways all the way to the Atlantic Ocean.

- Before oil, coal was the most important source of fuel. For many years huge amounts of coal have been mined from under the Appalachian Mountains in the eastern United States.

- The Golden Gate Bridge, near San Francisco, isn't really golden, but red, and it's always being painted. By the time the painters get to one end, the other needs paint again.

- If someone tells you they have some dollars, the dollars might be from the United States, Canada, New Zealand, or Australia. But if someone says they've got the bucks, that could only mean U.S. dollars.

- The United States has developed several distinctive and highly influential types of popular music: gospel, jazz, ragtime, blues, country and western, and rock and roll.

VIETNAM

The easternmost country in Southeast Asia is Vietnam. Four hundred miles long but only thirty miles wide, Vietnam is shaped like a giant *S*, which is why it's sometimes called the Dragon Land. Though in recent times many Vietnamese have moved to cities, the majority still live in the countryside and grow their main food crop, rice, sometimes bringing in two harvests a year. Their diet is supplemented by fish and shellfish from the South China Sea. Buddhism and Taoism are the major religions, and Confucianism is a predominant philosophy.

Vietnam can be divided into four distinct regions. The Annam Cordillera, a mountain range, extends from north to south through west-central Vietnam, while the Red River delta is in the north. The Mekong River delta (one of the richest rice-growing areas in the world) is in the southern part of the country, and the coastal plain lies in the east. Vietnam has a tropical monsoon climate, with hot winters in the south and cool winters in the north.

The capital city of Vietnam is Hanoi, a city in the north that has

French architecture and tree-lined boulevards. The French style is left over from the days of colonial occupation by France, who called Vietnam Cochin China. The combination of Cochin China, Cambodia, and Laos was known as Indochine, or French Indochina.

The Vietnamese people have a long history of fighting to preserve their independence. Three separate Mongol invasions in the thirteenth century were repulsed. The Chinese conquered the Vietnamese in 1407, but a national resistance movement drove the Chinese out in 1428. In the latter half of the nineteenth century, Vietnam was conquered by the French. After the Second World War, nationalists led by Ho Chi Minh declared Vietnam's independence, modeling their statement after the United States of America's Declaration of Independence. After many decades of war, Vietnam is once again an independent country.

Other Facts About Vietnam

- After the Second World War, the French tried to reclaim Vietnam but were finally defeated in 1954 after their forces were besieged at Dien Bien Phu.

- Influenced by its past as a French colony, restaurants in Vietnam often serve French cuisine, such as canard à l'orange.

- Vietnam's flag is red with a single yellow star.

- About one fourth of the country's total land area is cultivated.

- The major port of Vietnam is Haiphong.

- The primary mountain range, extending from north to south, is known as the Annam Cordillera.

- Besides Buddhism and Confucianism, many Vietnamese are followers of the Tao ("Way").

- The main city in the south, now called Ho Chi Minh City, was once known as Saigon.

- Centuries ago, the Vietnamese emperor lived in Hue, which is still known as the Imperial City.

- Other main cities are Annam, Than Hoa, Nam Dinh, Lao Cai, and Pleiku.

- Indigenous tribes, known as Montagnards, live deep in the highlands and have little contact with the more modern world of the cities.

- Much of the Vietnamese countryside is still recovering from the bombings and use of herbicides during the Vietnam War.

- The highest peak in Vietnam is Quang Ngai, at 10,761 feet, followed by Fan Si Pan, at 10,312 feet.

- The streets of Ho Chi Minh City are always crowded, and the best way to get around is by rickshaw or motorbike.

- During the Vietnam War, the North was separated from the South, and supplies from the North were sent along the Ho Chi Minh trail, deep in the mountainous jungles.

- In its early history, Vietnam enjoyed centuries of relative peace under the Ly Dynasty, established in 1009.

- Fishermen sail in boats known as sampans to catch fish in the South China Sea.

ZAIRE

Deepest, wildest Africa? You might well be thinking of the dense, mysterious, tropical jungles of a country like Zaire. Located on the equator, it is big enough to fill the entire eastern half of the United States. Zaire has so many different kinds of people that there are 200 different languages and dialects spoken. The four national languages are Swahili, Tshiluba, Lingala, and Kikongo. In addition to these, French is the lingua franca of government and administration.

Zaire occupies the heart of the Zaire River basin, which comprises about three fifths of the country's total area. The Zaire, with a length of about 2,900 miles, is one of the world's longest rivers, and flows through one of the world's most extensive tropical rain forests. In addition to its people, Zaire is home to an abundant variety of wildlife, including lions, gorillas, elephants, hippos, okapis, crocodiles, and pythons.

Only about three percent of Zaire's land area is under cultivation, such as the tea plantations in the Mitumba Mountains near

Zaire's eastern neighbor, Burundi. Many of Zaire's people live close to the land, depending for survival on the abundance of food and game in the rain forests and savannas. Mining, such as in the open-pit copper mine near Likasi, is a very important industry, since Zaire has some of the world's most important reserves of high-grade copper ore and cobalt, as well as substantial reserves of industrial diamonds, zinc, cadmium, gold, and silver.

Zaire was called the Belgian Congo when it was a colony ruled by King Leopold II of Belgium. The country became well known to Westerners over a hundred years ago, when an explorer named David Livingstone went on an expedition. A newspaperman named Henry Morton Stanley went looking for him. When after many travails, which he shared with readers around the world, Stanley finally found Livingstone in Tanzania, he uttered the famous phrase "Dr. Livingstone, I presume?" There is now a Stanley Falls near Kisangani, as well as a Livingstone Falls near the Atlantic Ocean.

Zaire won its independence under the leadership of Patrice Lumumba. Lumumba was a pan-African supporter who wanted Africa to be free of colonial rule by white European nations. Although he served as the prime minister of Zaire for a while, his government was unable to gain the support it needed. Lumumba was murdered in 1961 by the Katanga secessionist regime (supported by the Belgian colonialists). A simple man with a simple message of unity, his death horrified Africa and he is considered a hero of African nationalism. Since 1965, Zaire has been ruled by Mobutu Sese Seko.

Other Facts About Zaire

- Mount Margherita, at 16,821 feet, is Zaire's highest mountain. The Mountains of the Moon, also called the Ruwenzori Range, offer spectacular scenery.

- Almost all electricity in Zaire is produced by hydroelectric plants such as the dams at Inga, which send power all the way across the country to the copper mines at Kolwezi.

- Highland gorillas, among the most endangered species in the world, live in the eastern highlands near Uganda.

- The name Zaire refers to the country, its main river, and the money that the locals use. (In Zaire, it costs a few zaire to take a river trip on the Zaire!)

- Lake Tanganyika, lying in the western trough of the Great Rift Valley along Zaire's eastern boundary with Burundi and Tanzania, is one of the world's largest and deepest lakes. Other prominent lakes in Zaire are Lake Kivu and Lake Mai-Ndombe.

- Pygmies were the earliest settlers; it is thought that they arrived in Zaire in late Paleolithic times. They still live according to their ancient ways in places like the Ituri rain forest. Other indigenous peoples include the Luba, Mongo, Kongo, Lunda, and Kasai peoples.

- Zaire is the third-largest country in Africa, bordered on the west by the Congo; on the south by the Kasai River and Angola; on the southeast by Zambia; on the east by Tanzania, Burundi, Rwanda, and Uganda; and on the north by the Sudan and the Central African Republic.

- The capital of Zaire is Kinshasa, situated upriver from the tiny coastline on the Atlantic Ocean.

- The flag of Zaire is a field of green, with a yellow circle in which a hand holds a torch.

- The gross national product per capita of Zaire is among the lowest in the world.

- The Zaire River has many large tributaries, such as the Lualaba, the Lubudi, and the Lubilash. Watch out for crocodiles!

INDEX

C

Cabo San Lucas, 115
Cádiz, 115
caesars, 51, 101, 195
Cairo, 52
Cairo Museum, 51
Calabar, 131
Calcutta, 85
calendars, 70, 113
Caligula, 101
Callao, 141, 143
Calló, 176
Camagüey, 43
Cambodia, 23–26, 185, 209
Cambridge University, 199
camels, 4, 118, 131, 135
Canaanites, 118
Canada, 27–30
canals, 49–50, 53, 103–4, 124, 125, 138–40, 186, 207
canard à l'orange, 209
Canary Islands, 177
Canberra, 10
Cancún, 115
caning, 159
Cannes Film Festival, 56
Canterbury Plains, 126
Canton, 37
Cantonese, 35
Canute IV, 46, 48
Cape Agulhas, 165
Cape Colony, 167
Cape Horn, 6
Cape of Good Hope, 163, 166
Cape Town, 165
Capibaribe River, 21
Cappadocia, 193
Cardamomes Range, 24
Cardenas, 44
Carnaval, 20, 21
carpets, 5, 94
Cartier, Jacques, 30

Casablanca, 116
Casals, Pablo, 175
cashmere, 85
Caspian Sea, 91, 149, 150
cassava, 147
Castilian Spanish, 176
Castillo de la Punta, 44
Castle Hill, 74
castles, 47, 54, 62, 63, 107, 124
Castro, Fidel, 43
Catalán, 176
Catalonia, 176
Catherine the Great, 150
Catholic Church, 111, 145, 196–97
Caucasus Mountains, 148
cave art, 2
  and the Philippines, 146
  and South Korea, 169
  and Vietnam, 209
caviar, 150
Ceará, 21
Cebu, 145
Celebese, 86
Celebese Island, 90
Celebese Sea, 89
Celts, 196
cement, 94
Central Anatolian Plateau, 191
Central Havana, 43
Central Intelligence Agency (CIA), 152
ceramic ware, 76
Cervantes, Miguel, 175
Ceuta, 118
Cézanne, Paul, 55
chador, 93
chadris, 4
Chaing Mai, 188
champagne, 57
Champs Elysées, 55
Changi prison camp, 159–60

Channel Islands, 194–95
Chao Phraya River, 188
Charikar, 4
Charlemagne, 55
châteaus, 54
Checkpoint Charlie, 64
cheese, 57, 68, 125
Cheju Island, 169
Chekhov, Anton, 150
chemicals, 160
Chenab River, 135
Chengdu, 38
Chernobyl nuclear disaster, 179
Chesapeake Bay, 203
chewing gum, 159
Chiang Mai, 188
Chicago, Illinois, 202
Chichén Itzá, 113
Chiclayo, 141
Chile, 31–34
Chillan, 34
China, 35–40
Chin dynasty, 39
Chinese people, 146
chips (french fries), 199
Chitral, 136
Chogori, 135
Christianborg Palace (Copehagen), 47
Christianity, 46, 79, 86, 97, 101, 192, 193, 196–97
Christ the Redeemer statue, 20
chromium, 165
Chubut River, 7
Chulalongkorn, King, 187
Ch'u (region), 37
chullos, 18
Chup Plantation, 25
Churchill, Winston, 196, 198
CIA (Central Intelligence Agency), 152
Cidade de Minas, 21

Cienfuegos, 43
cigars, 42
Cinco de Mayo, 114–15
city-states, 66, 67
Civil War, 205
Clavell, James, 159–60
Cleopatra VII, 51–52
Clouds, The
    (Aristophanes), 65
Clyde River, 200
Clydesdale horses, 200
CN Tower (Toronto), 28
coal, 207
Cobán, 71
coca farming, 143
Cochabamba, 18
Cochin, 209
cocoa, 132
coconuts, 145, 147, 160
coffee, 14, 20, 110
Cold War, 151, 152
Colegio San Nicolás, 115
Coliseum, 101
Colombia, 139
Colón, 139
Colón Theater, 7
Colorado River, 203
Colossus of Rhodes, 68
Columbus, Christopher,
    42, 102, 138, 174,
    202, 204
commune system, 38–39
communism, 36–40, 43, 75,
    151–52, 153
compass, 102
concentration camps, 61
Confucianism, 36, 170, 208,
    210
Congo River, 182
Constantine I, 101, 192
Constantinople, 192
Constitution, U.S., 205–6
constitutional government,
    70
Cook, James, 12, 127

Cook Strait, 126
Copacabana beach, 20
Copenhagen, 47
Copernicus, Nikolaus, 103
copper, 32, 34, 114, 212,
    213
coral reefs, 9
cordillera, 23, 141
Cordillera de San Blas, 140
Cordillera Real, 16
Córdoba, 6, 173
Corniche, 156
Cornwall, England, 200
corroboree, 11
Corsica, 104
Cortés, Hernando, 113–14,
    115
Cossacks, 152, 153
Costa del Sol, 175–76
Costa Rica, 72, 140
Côte d'Azur, 57, 58
cotton, 132, 193, 205
country and western
    music, 207
cowboys, 5, 6, 34
cowrie shells, 130
Cozumel, 115
Crete, 65, 67
cricket, 160, 199
Crocodile River, 163
Crocodilopolis, 53
croissants, 57
cruzeiros, 20
Cuba, 41–44
Cubanacan, 42
Cuban Trogon, 44
Cumbrian Mountains, 195
Curitiba, 21
curried vegetables, 88
Cuzco, 142
Cymru, 196
Cyprus, 192
Cyrano de Bergerac
    (Rostand), 58
Cyrillic letters, 153

Cyrus the Great, 92
czars, 149–50
Czechoslovakia, 75

D

Dachau, 61
dahl, 122, 136
Daibutsu (Great Buddha),
    108
Dalai Lama, 37
Dalí, Salvador, 174
Damascus, Syria, 155
dams, 20, 50, 53, 101
Dangrek Mountains,
    23–24
Danish language, 47
Dante Alighieri, 103
Danube River, 14, 15,
    59–60, 73, 74
Dapsang (K2), 135
Dardanelles Strait, 190
Dar es-Salaam, 184
Darius the Great, 92
Darjeeling, 85
Darling River, 9
Darwin, 10
Dasht-e-Kavir, 91
Dasht-e-Lut, 91
dates, 156
Davao, Mindanao, 147
David, 140
David, Jacques-Louis, 55
David, King, 99
Dawson, Yukon
    Territories, 28
Day of the Dead, 72
Dayr el-Bahri, 51
Dead Sea, 97, 99
De Beer, Nicolaas and
    Diederick, 166
De Beers Consolidated
    Mines, Ltd., 166
Debrecen, 76

Declaration of Independence, 205, 206, 209
De Keukenhof Castle, 124
Delft, 125
Delhi, 84
Deli River, 89
Delphi, 67
Demilitarized Zone (DMZ), 169
democracy, 6, 33, 66, 70, 80, 83–84, 146, 174, 179
Democratic People's Republic of Korea, 168
Denmark, 45–48, 80, 179
departmento, 71
desalinated water, 154
Detroit, Michigan, 202
Detti Falls, 81
dharma, 84
diablada, 34
diamonds, 164, 165, 166
Dias, Bartholomeu, 166
Díaz, Porfirio, 115
Dickens, Charles, 199
dictatorships, 6, 33, 42–43, 60–61, 70, 92, 101, 151, 174
didgeridoo, 11
Dien Bien Phu, 209
dikes, 123
Dinesen, Isak, 46, 112
dirham, 118
diseases, 204
Divine Comedy, The (Dante Alighieri), 103
Dodoma, 184
dollars
  Australian, 11
  Canadian, 27
  Singapore, 160
  U.S., 207
Dome of the Rock, 97
Domingo, Plácido, 175
Donkin, Rufane, 167

Don Quixote (Cervantes), 175
dons, 199
Dortmund (Throtmanni), 63
Dostoyevsky, Fyodor, 150
Doubtful Sound, 126
Drake, Francis, 197
Drakensberg Mountains, 167
Dresden, 62–63
Dr. Zhivago (Pasternak), 153
drilling equipment, 160
drugs, 143, 187
druids, 195
Dulce River, 71
Dunedin, 128
Dunk, George Montague, second earl of Halifax, 29
Durban, 165
Durbar Square, 121
Düsseldorf, 64
Dutch East India Company, 86–87, 123–24
Dutch people, 123–25
  and Indonesia, 86–87, 88
  and South Africa, 163
dynamite, 181

E

Easter Island, 32
Eastern (Arabian) Desert, 49
Eastern Europe, 73
East Germany, 61–62, 63
East India Trading Company, 83
East Pakistan, 134
Ebola virus, 111
Edam, 125
Edinburgh, 128, 200
Edo Castle, 108
Egypt, 49–53, 98, 99

Eiffel, Alexandre-Gustave, 55
Eiffel Tower, 55
8½ (movie), 103
Eindhoven, 125
Einstein, Albert, 64
El Alamein, 53
Elat, 97
Elbe River, 62–63
Elburz Mountains, 91
Elder Edda, 79
electronics, 158, 187
Elephant Mountains, 24
El Estor, 71
Elfstedentocht, 125
El Greco, 174, 177
Elizabeth I, Queen of England, 197
Elizabeth II, Queen of England, 8
El Mirador, 71
El Misti, 142
El Niño, 143
El Salvador, 72
El Teniente, 34
Emerald Buddha, 186, 188
emperors, 36, 37, 40, 60, 101, 149–50
England, 195, 196–98
English Channel, 199
English language, 83, 93, 110, 130, 147, 159, 184, 196
erhu, 38
Erie Canal, 207
Eriksson, Leif, 79
Erik the Red, 79
Erzurum, 191
Eskimos, 28
Essen, 64
estancias, 5
Esterhazy Palace, 76
Esztergom, 76
Euripides, 65
European Russia, 148–49

maghreb, 118
magic, 34
Magna Carta, 197
magnesite, 193
Magyar language, 73
Magyars, 73, 74
Mahabharata, 84
Mahabharat Lekh, 122
maharajahs, 85
maharanis, 85
Mahatma, 83
Mahfouz, Naguib, 53
Mahler, Gustav, 14
Mahmud of Ghazna, 3
Maiduguri, 132
Maimana, 4
Major University of San
    Simon, 18
Malang, 90
Malay language, 87, 90, 159
Malay Peninsula, 158
Malay people, 146
Malecon, 43, 44
Malla dynasty, 121
Malvina Islands, 6
Mama Ocllo, 18
Manaus, 20
Manchu dynasty, 40
Manchuria, 168
mandala, 89
Mandarin Chinese
    language, 35, 159
mandarins, 36
Mandela, Nelson, 164
mandi, 90
Manet, Édouard, 55
mangrove swamps, 43–44,
    158
Manila, 145–46, 147
Manisa, 193
Manitoba province, 28
Manju-Patan, 120–21, 122
Mansfield, Katherine, 128
Manukau Harbour, 128
Maori people, 127, 128

Mao Zedong, 36
Mapuche people, 34
Marathon, 66
Marcal River, 76
Marc Antony, 51–52, 101
Marcos, Ferdinand, 146
Mardan, 136
Mar del Plata, 7
Marie Antoinette, 55–56
mariner's compass, 102
Maritz, Gerrit, 167
marks, 62
Marlboroug, 128
Marquesas, 32
Marrakech, 116, 118
Marsabit, 111
"Marseillaise, The," 57
Marseille, 57–58
marshes, 43–44
marsupials, 10
Martí, José, 42, 43
Marx, Karl, 150–51
Marxism, 33
Masada, 99
Masai Mara, 111
Masai people, 111, 183
Masbate, 145
Mashhad, 94
Masjid-i-Shah Cheragh, 93
Mas River, 89
Massif Central, 54
Mastroianni, Marcello, 103
Mata Hari, 90
Matanzas province, 43–44
matches, 181
mate, 7
mathematics, 65, 113
Mathias Corvinus, King,
    76–77
Matisse, Henri, 55
Mato Grosso, 22
Mauryan Empire, 134
Mauryas, 83
Mayan ruins, 70–71
Mayans, 69–71, 113

May Day (May 1), 151
Mazar-e-Sharif, 2
Mazatlán, 115
Mecca, 93, 155, 156
Medan, Sumatra, 89
Medes, 92
Medici family, 103
Medina, 155
Mediterranean Sea, 49, 57,
    105, 118
mein, 35
Meknes, 117
Mekong River, 23, 25, 185,
    208
Melbourne, 9, 11, 12
melting pot, 201
Merchant of Venice, The
    (Shakespeare), 117
Merlion statue, 161
Meru people, 111
"metal horse," 38
Mexico, 113–15
Mexico City, 114
Michaelangelo, 102
microscopes, 124
Middle Ages, 55, 102, 105
Milan, 104
Milford Sound, 126
military junta, 33, 42–43
milk, 136, 137
minarets, 93
Minas Gerais, 20, 21
Mindanao, 145
Mindoro, 145
Ming dynasty, 38
Minna, 132
Minos, King, 67
Minotaur, 67
mint tea, 116
miombo woodlands, 184
Miskolc, 76
Mississippi-Missouri-Red
    Rock River, 203
Mistral, Gabriela, 33
Mitumba Mountains, 211

Napier, 128
Naples, 104
Napoléon Bonaparte, 56, 150
Napoleonic Wars, 180
Napoleon III, 114–15
napoleons, 57
Narayani area, 121
NASA, 202
Nasser, Gamel, 49–50
Natal province, 166, 167
National Botanic Gardens, 166
nationalist China, 39, 40
Nationalist Party, 87
National Theater, 74
National Water Carrier system, 96
Native Americans, 203, 204, 206
   Aztecs, 114
   in Canada, 27–28
   Incas, 17, 18, 141, 142, 144
   in Chile, 34
   in Cuba, 42
   in Guatemala, 70
   Mayans, 69–71, 113
   in Panama, 138
natural gas, 94, 130, 155
Navajo, 204
Nazareth, 97
Nazca people, 144
Nazis, 60–61, 97, 124
Ndebele people, 164
Neanderthal man, 64
Neanderthal valley, 64
Neapolitans, 104
Near East, 96
Nefertiti, 51
Negev Desert, 96
Nepal, 119–22
Nero, 101
Neruda, Pablo, 33
Netherlands, 123–25, 158

Neuquén, 7
Neuquén River, 7
New Amsterdam, 123, 125
Newcastle, 10
New Delhi, 84
Newfoundland, 29–30
New Guinea, 86
New Havana, 43
New Orleans, Louisiana, 202
New South Wales, 10, 11
New Testament, 98–99
Newton, Isaac, 199
New World, 102, 204
New York City, New York, 123, 125, 201, 202, 206–7
New Zealand, 126–28
Ngadda River, 132
Nguni language, 164
Niagara Falls, 29
Nicaragua, 72
Nice, 57
Nigeria, 129–32
Niger River, 129, 131
Nike, 57
Nile River, 50, 52, 53, 182
Ninety Mile Beach, 126
nirvana, 122
Nissum Fjord, 45
nitrates, 34
Noah's Ark, 190
Nobel, Alfred, 181
Nobel Prize, 33, 46, 53, 79, 153, 164, 181
Noh, 108
Nok people, 130
nomads, 111, 117, 118, 183
noodles, 35, 103, 160
Noriega, Manuel, 139
Normandy, 57
Normans, 195
Norrköping, 181
Norse explorers, 29
Norse gods, 45, 48, 79

Norse language, 79
Norse legends, 79
North America, 202
Northern Ireland, 196
Northern Territory, 10
North German Confederation, 60
North Korea, 168, 169, 171
North Sea, 46
Northwest Territories, 29
Norway, 80, 180
Notre Dame, 55
Nova Scotia province, 29
nuclear power, 179
nuclear weapons, 107, 127, 151, 171
nuevo sol, 144
Nullarbor Plain, 8
nuraghi, 104
Nyerere, Julius, 184

O

oasis, 156, 157
Oaxaca, 115
Occidental, 44
Octavius, 52, 101
Odense, 47–48
Odense River, 47–48
Odin, 45, 48, 79
Odysseus, 68
Odyssey (Homer), 68
Ogbomosho, 131
oil, 92, 93, 94, 114, 154, 155–56, 157, 160
Ojos del Salado, 31
Oland Island, 181
Old Havana, 43, 44
Old Jerusalem, 97, 98–99
Old Norse, 80
Old Testament, 98–99
Olduvai Gorge, 184
olive oil, 68
olives, 68, 117

samisen, 107
Samos, 68
sampans, 210
samurai, 107
San (Bushman), 167
San Adreas Island, 71
San Fernando, 34
San Francisco, California, 202, 207
San Francisco de Paula, 44
sangria, 176
San Luis, 44
San Luis Valley, 44
Sanskrit, 83
Santa Claus, 125
Santa Cruz, 18
Santa Maria volcano, 71
Santiago, 32–33
Santo Tomás de Castillia, 71
São Paulo, 21
Sapele, 131
Sapporo, 106
Saratov, 153
sarcophagi, 51
Sardinia, 104
sarongs, 88, 90
Saskatchewan province, 28
Saud, Abdul Aziz ibn, 155
Saud dynasty, 155, 156
Saudi Arabia, 93, 154–57
Saul, King, 136
savannas, 129, 163
sawmilling, 131
schillings, 14
Schoenberg, Arnold, 14
Schubert, Franz, 14
Scotland, 195–96, 200
Scottish Free Church, 128
Scriabin, Aleksandr, 150
scribes, 50
sculpture
    bronze, 131
    French, 58
    Greek, 66, 68
Sea of Galilee, 97

Sea of Japan, 168, 172
Sea of Marmara, 190
Sebek, 53
Sechura Desert, 144
Second World War, 63
    Britain and, 198
    Germany and, 60, 61, 64
    Hungary and, 74, 75
    Japan and, 107, 109
    Netherlands and, 124
    Philippines and, 145–46
    South Korea and, 169–70
    Soviet Union and, 151
Segovia, Andrés, 175
Seine River, 54, 55, 58
Semang people, 189
Semarang, Java, 89
Semarang River, 89
Sendero Luminoso, 143
Seoul, 169–70, 171
Serengeti National Park, 183
sertao, 22
Service, Robert W., 28
Seven Great Temples of Nara, 108
Seven Wonders of the Ancient World, 68
Seven Wonders of the World, 52
Sevilla, 173
sewage systems, 101
Shah Cheragh shrine, 93
Shah Jahan, 135–36
shahs, 92
Shah Square, 94
Shakespeare, William, 45, 47, 108, 117, 184, 199–200
Shalimar Gardens, 135–36
shamans, 122
shan, 39
Shandong province, 39
Shanghai, 37
Sharif, Omar, 53

Shedet, 53
sheep, 4, 6, 12, 126
shekels, 99
Sherpa, 120
sherry, 175
Shetland Islands, 81
Shetland ponies, 81
Shi'a Islam, 2, 94
Shi'ite Muslims, 92–93
shillings
    Kenyan, 112
    Tanzanian, 184
Shintoism, 106
Shinto people, 106
Shiraz, 92
Shiva, 84, 121
Shivaratri festival, 121
Shōgun (Clavell), 159–60
shoguns, 108
Shostakovitch, Dmitry, 150
Shrine of La Tirana, 34
Shrivijaya Empire, 89
shwarma, 157
Siam, 186
Siamese cats, 186
Siberia, 149, 152, 153
Sichuan Opera, 38
Sichuan University, 38
Sicily, 105
Sierra Madre, 114
Sierra Maestra, 41
Sihanouk, Norodom, 24–25
Sikhism, 85, 135
Sikhs, 135
Sikkim Himalayas, 85
silk, 35
silk cotton, 26
silver, 5, 7, 114, 115, 153, 212
Sinai Peninsula, 49, 52, 98
Sindhi language, 133
Sindh region, 135
Singapore, 158–61
Sinkep, 90
siroccos, 117

T

Wakhan Corridor, 1
Wales, 196, 198–99
Wall Street, 201
waltzing mathilda, 12
Warri, 132
Washington, D.C., 206
Wat Chedi Luang, 188
water buffalo, 136, 137
water taxis, 103–4
Wat Po, 187
wats (temples), 188
wayang kulit, 88
weapons, 98
weaving, 132, 143, 144
Webber, Andrew Lloyd, 7
Weber, Carl Maria von, 63
Weimar constitution, 60
welfare systems, 45, 128,
    179
Wellington, 128
Welsh language, 196
Weser River, 63
West Bank, 98
Western Australia, 11
Western Roman Empire,
    104
Western Wall, 97
West Germany, 62
Westminster Abbey, 200
West Pakistan, 134
whaling, 128
Whirling Dervishes, 192
White Cliffs of Dover, 199
Wiener schnitzel, 14
Wilhelm, Kaiser, 60
Wilhelm I, King, 60
William IV, King, 11
Wimbledon, 199
windmills, 123
wine, 33, 57, 76
Winnipeg, Manitoba, 28
Winter Palace, 150
Witwatersrand, 163, 165
won, 171
wool, 78, 126, 128, 144

alpaca, 18, 32
    of Karakul sheep, 4
Woolloomooloo Bay, 12
Woolongong, 10
woomera, 12
work camps, 151
World War I. *See* First
    World War
World War II. *See* Second
    World War
Wuhan, 38

X

Xhosa people, 163, 164, 166

Y

Yafo, 96
Yafo Gate, 97
yaks, 4, 120
Yangtze River, 38
Yellow River, 39
Yellow Sea, 39, 172
Yemen, 156
yen, 108
Yepes, Narciso, 175
yeshivas, 98
yeti, 119
Yi Dynasty, 169
yin and yang, 39, 171
Yokohama, 106
Yorkshire, England, 199
Yorkshire pudding, 199
Yorubaland, 131
Yoruba people, 129, 131
Young Turks, 191
yuan, 38
Yucatán Peninsula, 113
Yugoslavia, 75
Yukon Territories, 28
Yunnan province, 38
yurts, 39

Z

Zagros Mountains, 91
Zaire, 211–13
zaire, 213
Zaire River, 211, 213
Zambezi River, 182
Zanzibar, 183, 184
Zapata Peninsula, 44
zapata sparrow, 44
Zaria, 131
Zealand, 45
Zen Buddhism, 106–7
zero, 113
Zeus, 67
Zimbabwe, 162
Zionist movement, 97
Zoroaster, 4
Zoroastrianism, 4
Zulu people, 163, 164, 167
Zwinger Palace, 63

Carmen Sandiego™ Challenges Kids to Discover the World!

Ages 9 & up
USA Geography and Regional Cultures
WIN/MAC CD-ROM

Ages 9 & up
World Geography and Cultures
WIN/MAC CD-ROM

Save $20

Purchase New Editions of both "Where in the World is Carmen Sandiego?"™ AND "Where in the USA is Carmen Sandiego?"™ CD-ROM geography games, and get $20 back.*

To receive $20 rebate by mail:

❶ Complete this **original** rebate coupon (no photocopies, please);

❷ Include the **original** sales receipt(s) indicating your qualifying purchases of **each** New Edition;

❸ Complete product registration cards for **both** products.

❹ **Mail all items to:**
Carmen Clue Book Offer
P.O. Box 52929, Dept. 2616
Phoenix, AZ 85072-2929

Name _____ Address _____

City _____ State _____ Zip _____ Daytime Phone ( ) _____